C and Python Applications

Embedding Python Code in C Programs, SQL Methods, and Python Sockets

Philip Joyce

Apress®

C and Python Applications: Embedding Python Code in C Programs, SQL Methods, and Python Sockets

Philip Joyce
Crewe, UK

ISBN-13 (pbk): 978-1-4842-7773-7   ISBN-13 (electronic): 978-1-4842-7774-4
https://doi.org/10.1007/978-1-4842-7774-4

Managing Director, Apress Media LLC: Welmoed Spahr
Acquisitions Editor: Celestin Suresh John
Development Editor: James Markham
Coordinating Editor: Divya Modi

Cover designed by eStudioCalamar

Cover image designed by Pixabay

Distributed to the book trade worldwide by Springer Science+Business Media New York, 1 New York Plaza, New York, NY 10004. Phone 1-800-SPRINGER, fax (201) 348-4505, e-mail orders-ny@springer-sbm.com, or visit www.springeronline.com. Apress Media, LLC is a California LLC and the sole member (owner) is Springer Science + Business Media Finance Inc (SSBM Finance Inc). SSBM Finance Inc is a **Delaware** corporation.

For information on translations, please e-mail booktranslations@springernature.com; for reprint, paperback, or audio rights, please e-mail bookpermissions@springernature.com.

Apress titles may be purchased in bulk for academic, corporate, or promotional use. eBook versions and licenses are also available for most titles. For more information, reference our Print and eBook Bulk Sales web page at http://www.apress.com/bulk-sales.

Any source code or other supplementary material referenced by the author in this book is available to readers on GitHub via the book's product page, located at www.apress.com/9781484277737. For more detailed information, please visit http://www.apress.com/source-code.

Printed on acid-free paper

Table of Contents

About the Author ix

About the Technical Reviewer xi

Acknowledgments xiii

Introduction xv

Chapter 1: Python Programming 1

Definition of Variables 1

    Real (Float) Numbers 5

    Characters 6

Reading in Data 6

Arrays 8

    Inserting into an Array 9

    Deleting (Removing) from an Array 10

    Searching 10

    Updating an Array 11

    Appending to an Array 11

Strings 12

Lists 14

    Reading Entries in a List 15

    Updating a List 16

    Deleting an Element from List 16

    Appending to a List 16

Dictionaries 17

    Creating a Dictionary 17

    Appending to a Dictionary 17

    Amending a Dictionary 18

Deleting from a Dictionary 19

Searching Through a Dictionary 19

Tuples 20

Creating a Tuple 21

Concatenating Two Tuples 22

Creating Nested Tuples 22

Creating Repeated Tuples 22

Converting a List or a String into a Tuple 23

Creating Single-Element Tuple 23

Reading Tuple 23

Searching Within a Tuple 23

Deleting a Tuple 24

Using Tuple to Create Variables 24

If Then Else 25

Loops (For and While) 26

For Loops 26

While Loops 28

Switches 29

Arithmetic Operations Using Numpy 30

Numpy Calculations 34

Mathematical Graph Functions 38

User-Written Functions 43

File Access 45

Regressions 52

Summary 57

Exercises 57

Chapter 2: C Programming 59

C Program Format 59

Adding Two Numbers 60

Multiply and Divide Two Numbers 62

For Loops 63

Do While Loops 65

Switch Instruction 66

If Else 67

If Else If 68

Data Arrays 70

Functions 81

Strings 86

Structures 88

Size of Variables 91

Goto Command 92

Common Mathematical and Logical Symbols 93

File Access 94

    Student Records File 95

Summary 105

Exercises 106

Chapter 3: SQL in C 107

Review of SQL and SQLite 107

Creating the Database 108

Creating a Table 110

Inserting Rows 113

    Insert a Preset Row 113

    Inserting a User-Entered Row 114

Selecting Rows 117

    Selecting a Row Preset 117

    Selecting All Rows 120

    Selecting Rows by Age 122

Amending Rows 125

Deleting Rows 128

Summary 130

Exercises 130

Chapter 4: SQL in Python **131**

    Review of SQL 131

        Create a Table 133

        Mechanism for Inserting a Row 134

        Update a Row 139

        Delete a Row 148

        Read a Table 149

    Summary 150

    Exercises 150

Chapter 5: Embedded Python **151**

    Basic Mechanism 151

    Plot a 2D Line 153

    Plot Two 2D Lines 155

    Plot Trigonometric Curves 158

    Enter Data to Plot 160

    2D Center of Mass Plot 170

    Histograms 177

    Importing a Picture 179

    Summary 181

    Exercise 181

Chapter 6: Sockets **183**

    A Closer Look at Sockets 183

    Basic Client-Server 185

    Server-Client Pair to Send-Receive a File 187

    Threaded Programs 191

    Closing Down a Threaded Server 194

    Chat Programs 197

    Summary 199

    Exercise 199

Appendix A: Answers to Examples **201**

    Chapter 1 201

    Chapter 2 206

    Chapter 3 212

    Chapter 4 219

    Chapter 5 223

    Chapter 6 228

Index **231**

About the Author

Philip Joyce has 28 years of experience as a software engineer, working on control of steel production, control of oil refineries, communications software (pre-Internet), office products (server software), and computer control of airports. He programs in Assembler, COBOL, Coral 66, C, and C++ with SQL. He served as a mentor to new graduates in the Ferranti Company. He obtained an MSc in computational physics (including augmented matrix techniques and Monte Carlo techniques using Fortran) from Salford University in 1996. He is also a chartered physicist and a member of the Institute of Physics (member of the Higher Education Group).

About the Technical Reviewer

 **Swathi Sutrave** is a self-professed tech geek. She has been a subject matter expert for several different programming languages, including Python, C, and SQL, for corporations, startups, and universities.

Acknowledgments

Thanks to my wife, Anne, for her support, my son Michael, and my daughter Katharine. All three have mathematics degrees. Thanks to everyone on the Apress team who helped me with the publication of this, my third book.

Introduction

The C and Python programming languages are important languages in many computer applications. This book will demonstrate how to use the C and Python languages to write applications in SQL. It will demonstrate how to embed a Python program within a C program. Finally, the reader will learn how to create Python socket programs which can communicate with each other on different computers (these are called "sockets").

A basic familiarity with mathematics is assumed along with some experience of the basics of computer programs. The first two chapters review the basics of C and Python. The chapters following these are grouped into SQL techniques, embedded Python, and sockets applications. There are exercises in each chapter with answers and suggested code at the end of the book.

CHAPTER 1

Python Programming

This is the first of two chapters in which you'll review both Python and C programming languages. A basic understanding of computing and what programs are about is assumed although no prior knowledge of either Python or C is needed.

In this chapter, we will start with the basics of Python. This will include how items used in a program are stored in the computer, basic arithmetic formats, handling strings of characters, reading in data that the user can enter on the command line, etc. Then we will work up to file access on the computer, which will lead us up to industrial/commercial-level computing by the end of the book.

If you don't already have a Python development environment on your computer, you can download it and the Development Kit, free of charge, from `www.python.org/downloads/`. Another way you can access Python is by using Visual Studio. Again, a version of this can be downloaded.

Definition of Variables

This section looks at the different types of store areas that are used in Python. We refer to these store areas as "variables." The different types can be numbers (integers or decimals), characters, and different types of groups of these (strings, arrays, dictionaries, lists, or tuples).

In these examples, you can go to the command line and enter "Python" which starts up the Python environment and produces ">>>" as the prompt for you to enter Python code.

© Philip Joyce 2022
P. Joyce, *C and Python Applications*, https://doi.org/10.1007/978-1-4842-7774-4_1

In Python, unlike C, you don't define the variable as a specific type. The different types are integer, floating point, character, string, etc. The type is assigned when you give the variable a value. So try the following code:

```
>>> a1 = 51
>>> print(type(a1))
We get the output
<class 'int'>
>>>
```

Here we are defining a variable called "a1" and we are assigning the integer value 51 to it.

We then call the function "print" with the parameter "type" and "a1" and we get the reply "class 'int'". "type" means that we want to display whether the variable is an integer, floating point, character, string, etc.

We can now exit the Python environment by typing "quit()".

We will now perform the same function from a program.

Create a file called "typ1a.py".

Then enter the following two lines of Python code:

```
a1=51
print(type(a1))
```

Now on the command line, enter "python typ1a.py".

And you should get the output

```
<class 'int'>
```

which is the same as our first example.

This is just demonstrating the equivalence of the two methods.

Obviously, if you want to run a program with many lines of code and possibly run it many times, then having the code in a file is more efficient.

We can demonstrate different data types being stored in the same variable using the following code:

```
a1=51
print(type(a1))

a1=51.6
print(type(a1))
```

2

```
a1='51'
print(type(a1))
```

When we run this, we get

```
<class 'int'>
<class 'float'>
<class 'str'>
```

The 51 entered is an int. The 51.6 is a float (decimal) type, and '51' is a string.
We can make the results a little clearer if we use print("a1 is", type(a1)).
So our program now reads

```
a1=51
print("a1 is",type(a1))
```

```
a1=51.6
print("a1 is",type(a1))
```

```
a1='51'
print("a1 is",type(a1))
```

and the output is

```
a1 is <class 'int'>
a1 is <class 'float'>
a1 is <class 'str'>
```

We can put a comment on our line of code by preceding it with the "#" character.

```
a1='51' #assign string containing 51 to variable a1
print("a1 is",type(a1)) # print the type assigned to a1
```

Some simple arithmetic operations are shown in the following.
The following code is held in the file "arith1.py":

```
arith1a.py
```

Initialize the variables v1, v2, v3, and v4 with integer values.

```
v1= 2
v2 = 4
v3 = 7
v4 = 8
```

Add v1 to v2 and store the result in v5.

```
v5 = v1 + v2
print(v5)
```

The result is

```
6
```

You can combine the adding with the print as follows:

```
print(v1+v2)
```

Giving the same answer:

```
6
```

Now a subtraction:

```
v6 = v4 - v3
print(v6)
giving
1
```

Now a multiplication:

```
v7 = v4 * v3

print(v7)
giving
56
```

Now a division:

```
v8 = v4 / v1
print(v8)
giving
4.0
```

```
v10 = v3 % v2 # the % sign means show the remainder of the division
print(v10)
gives
3
```

Raise by the power 2.

```
v11 = v2 ** 2
print(v11)
gives
16
```

Raise to the power held in variable v1.

Here v2 contains 4 and v1 contains 2.

```
v11 = v2 ** v1
print(v11)
gives
16
```

Show how Python obeys the rules of BODMAS (BIDMAS).

Here v2 contains 4, v1 contains 2, v3 contains 7, and v4 contains 8.

```
v11 = v1 + v2 * v4 - v3 # show BODMAS
print(v11)
gives
27
```

Show how Python obeys the normal algebra rules.

```
v11 = (v1 + v2) * (v4 - v3)
print(v11)
gives
6
```

Real (Float) Numbers

This type of number contains a decimal point. So, for the following assignments

```
V1 = 2
V2 = 3.5
V3 = 5.1
V4 = 6.75
```

we get

```
print(type(V1))
<class 'int'>
print(type(V2))
<class 'float'>
print(type(V3))
<class 'float'>
print(type(V4))
<class 'float'>
```

Characters

In Python, you can also assign characters to locations, for example:

```
c1 = 'a'
print(type(c1))
produces
<class 'str'>
```

which means that c1 is classed as a string.

Now that we know what different types of variables we can have, we will look at how we use them.

Reading in Data

Now that we can display a message to the person running our program, we can ask them to type in a character, then read the character, and print it to the screen. This section looks at how the user can enter data to be read by the program.

If we type in the command

```
vara = input()
```

the computer waits for the user to type in data.

So if you now enter r5, the computer stores r5 in the variable vara.

You can check this by printing the contents of vara by typing

```
print(vara)
```

which prints

r5

We can make this more explicit by using

```
print("data typed in is:-", vara)
giving
data typed in is:-r5
```

You can also make the entry command clearer to the user by entering

```
varb=input("enter some data to be stored in varb")
```

Then, again we can explicitly print out the contents

```
print("data typed in is:-", varb)
giving
data typed in is:-r5
```

You have to use int(input) to enter an integer.
Otherwise, it is a string (one or more characters), for example:

```
n = int(input('Enter a number: '))
you enter 4
 >>> print(type(n))
<class 'int'>
```

```
# Program to check input
# type in Python

num = input ("Enter number :")
print(num)
#You could enter 5 here and it would store 5 as a string and not as a
number
>>> print(num)
5
>>> print ("type of number", type(num))
type of number <class 'str'>
>>>
```

```
#entering a float number (type 'float' before the 'input' command)
n = float(input('Enter a number: '))
Enter a number: 3.8
>>> print(type(n))
<class 'float'>
>>> print(n )
3.8
```

Now that we can enter data manually into the program, we will look at groups of data.

Arrays

An array is an area of store which contains a number of items. So from our previous section on integers, we can have a number of integers defined together with the same label. Python does not have a default type of array, although we have different types of array.

So we can have an array of integers called "firstintarr" with the numbers 2, 3, 5, 7, 11, and 13 in it. Each of the entries is called an "element," and the individual elements of the array can be referenced using its position in the array. The position is called the "index." The elements in the array have to be of the same type. The type is shown at the beginning of the array.

The array mechanism has to be imported into your program, as shown as follows:

```
from array import *
firstintarr = array('i', [2,3,5,7,11])
```

The 'i' in the definition of firstintarr means that the elements are integers.

And we can reference elements of the array using the index, for example:

```
v1 = firstintarr[3]
print(v1)
```

This outputs

```
7
```

We can also define floating point variables in an array by replacing the "i" by "f" in the definition of the array.

So we can define

```
firstfloatarr = array( 'f', [0.2,4.3,21.9,7.7])
```

And we can now write

```
varfloat1 = firstfloatarr[1]
print(varfloat1)
```

This will store 4.3 into varfloat1.

The array mechanism has to be imported into your program.

So at the start of each program, you need to include the code

```
from array import *
```

Once we have our array, we can insert, delete, search, or update elements into the array.

Array is a container which can hold a fix number of items, and these items should be of the same type. Most of the data structures make use of arrays to implement their algorithms. The following are the important terms to understand the concept of array:

- Insert

- Delete (remove)

- Search

- Update

- Append

Let's review them now.

Inserting into an Array

The following code is in the file array3.py:

```
from array import *

myarr = array('i', [2,3,5,7,11])

myarr.insert(1,13) # this inserts 13 into position 1 of the array (counting
from 0)

for x in myarr:
 print(x)
```

This outputs

2
13
3
5
7
11

Deleting (Removing) from an Array

The following code is in the source code file array4.py:

array4.py

```python
from array import *

myarr = array('i', [2,3,5,7,11])

myarr.remove(2) # this removes the element containing 2 from the array

for x in myarr:
 print(x)
```

This outputs

3
5
7
11

Searching

The following code is in the file array5.py:

```python
from array import *

myarr = array('i', [2,3,5,7,11])

print (myarr.index(3))#this finds the index of the array which contains 3
```

This outputs

```
1
```

Updating an Array

The following code is in the file array6.py:

array6.py

```
from array import *

myarr = array('i', [2,3,5,7,11])

myarr[2] = 17) #this updates element 2 with 17

for x in myarr:
 print(x)
```

This outputs

```
2
3
17
7
11
```

Appending to an Array

The following code is in the file array9a.py:

array9a.py

```
from array import *

myarr = array('i', [2,3,5,7,11])

for x in myarr:
 print(x)

new = int(input("Enter an integer: "))
myarr.append(new)
print(myarr)
```

This outputs

```
2
3
5
7
11

Enter an integer: 19

array('i', [2, 3, 5, 7, 11, 19])
```

This section has shown the "array" use in Python.

Strings

Strings are similar to the character arrays we discussed in the previous section. They are defined within quotation marks. These can be either single or double quotes. We can specify parts of our defined string using the slice operator ([ ] and [:]). As with character arrays, we can specify individual elements in the string using its position in the string (index) where indexes start at 0.

We can concatenate two strings using "+" and repeat the string using "*".

We cannot update elements of a string – they are immutable. This means that once they are created, they cannot be amended.

The following code:

```
firststring = 'begin'
print(firststring)
gives
begin
```

The following code:

```
one = 1
two = 2
three = one + two
print(three)
#gives
3
```

12

The following code:

```
first = " first "
second= "second"
concat = first + " " + second
print(concat)
#gives
first   second
print("concat: %s" % concat)
gives
concat:  first   second
The following code is in the file tst13a.py
secondstring = "second string"
print(secondstring.index("o")) #gives
3
print(secondstring.count("s")) # count the number of s characters in string
gives
2

print(secondstring[2:9]) # prints slice of string from 2 to 9 giving

cond st
print(secondstring[2:9:1]) #  The general form is [start:stop:step] giving

cond st
print(secondstring[::-1]) # Reverses the string giving

gnirts dnoces

splitup = secondstring.split(" ")
print(splitup) #gives
['second', 'string']
```

Strings are immutable, so if we tried

```
second= "second"
second[0]="q"
```

we get

```
Traceback (most recent call last):
  File "<stdin>", line 1, in <module>
TypeError: 'str' object does not support item assignment
```

indicating that we tried to update something (a string in this case) which is immutable.

Lists

Lists are similar to arrays and strings, in that you define a number of elements, which can be specified individually using the index. With lists, however, the elements can be of different types, for example, a character, an integer, and a float.

The following code is in the file alist7.py:

```
firstlist = ['k', 97 ,56.42, 64.08, 'bernard']
```

We specify the elements within square brackets.

We can then access individual elements in the list using the index (starting from 0), for example:

```
print(firstlist[0])
gives
k
print(firstlist[1:3])
gives
[97, 56.42]
```

We can amend an element in a list.

```
firstlist[3] = 'plj'
print(firstlist)
giving
['k', 97, 56.42, 'plj', 'bernard']
```

We can delete an element from a list.

```
del firstlist[3]
print(firstlist)
giving
['k', 97, 56.42, 'bernard']
```

We can append an element to the list.

```
firstlist.append(453.769)
print(firstlist)
giving
['k', 97, 56.42, 'bernard', 453.769]
```

Reading Entries in a List

The following code is held in the file alist1a.py:

alist1a.py

```
list1 = ['first', 'second', 'third']
list2 = [1, 2, 3, 4, 5 ]

print ("list1: ", list1)
print ("list1[0]: ", list1[0])
print ("list2: ", list2)
print ("list2[3]: ", list2[3])
print ("list2[:3]: ", list2[:3])
print ("list2[2:]: ", list2[2:])
print ("list2[1:3]: ", list2[1:3])
```

This outputs

```
list1:  ['first', 'second', 'third']
list1[0]:  first
list2:  [1, 2, 3, 4, 5]
list2[3]:  4
list2[:3]:  [1, 2, 3]
list2[2:]:  [3, 4, 5]
list2[1:3]:  [2, 3]
```

Updating a List

The following code is held in the file alist2a.py:

```
alist2a.py

list1 = [1, 2, 3, 4, 5 ]

print ("list1: ", list1)

list1[1] = 26 #update the second item (counting from zero)

print ("updated list1: ", list1)
```

This outputs

```
list1:   [1, 2, 3, 4, 5]
updated list1:   [1, 26, 3, 4, 5]
```

Deleting an Element from List

The following code is held in the file alist3a.py:

```
alist3a.py
list1 = [1,2,3,4,5,6]
print (list1)
del list1[4]
print ("Updated list1 : ", list1)
```

This outputs

```
[1, 2, 3, 4, 5, 6]
Updated list1 :   [1, 2, 3, 4, 6]
```

Appending to a List

The following code is held in the file alist4aa.py:

```
alist4aa.py
list2 = [10,11,12,13,14,15]
print (list2)
```

```
new = int(input("Enter an integer: "))
list2.append(new)
print(list2)
```

This outputs (if you enter 489)

```
[10, 11, 12, 13, 14, 15]
```

```
Enter an integer: 489
```

```
[10, 11, 12, 13, 14, 15, 489]
```

This has shown the use of lists.

Dictionaries

Dictionaries contain a list of items where one item acts as a key to the next. The list is unordered and can be amended. The key-value relationships are unique. Dictionaries are mutable.

Creating a Dictionary

In the first example, we create an empty dictionary. In the second, we have entries.

```
firstdict = {}
```

or

```
firstdict ={'1':'first','two':'second','my3':'3rd'}
```

Appending to a Dictionary

The following code is held in the file adict1a.py:

```
adict1a.py
#create the dictionary
adict1 = {'1':'first','two':'second','my3':'3rd'}

print (adict1)
```

```
print (adict1['two'])   # in the dictionary 'two' is the key to 'second'

adict1[4] = 'four' # we want to add another value called 'four' whose key
is 4

print (adict1)

print (len(adict1)) #this will print the number of key-value pairs
```

This outputs

```
{'1': 'first', 'two': 'second', 'my3': '3rd'}
second
{'1': 'first', 'two': 'second', 'my3': '3rd', 4: 'four'}
4
```

If we want to add value whose key is dinsdale, then we specify it as 'dinsdale'.
So

```
adict1['dinsdale'] = 'doug'
print (adict1)
```

outputs

```
{'1': 'first', 'two': 'second', 'my3': '3rd', 4: 'four', 'dinsdale': 'doug'}
```

Amending a Dictionary

The following code is held in the file adict2a.py.
    This amends the value whose key is 'two' to be '2nd'.

```
adict2a.py
adict1 = {'1':'first','two':'second','my3':'3rd'}

adict1['two'] = '2nd'

print(adict1)
```

This outputs

```
{'1': 'first', 'two': '2nd', 'my3': '3rd'}
```

Deleting from a Dictionary

The following code is held in the file adict3a.py:

```
adict3a.py
adict1 = {'1':'first','two':'second','my3':'3rd'}
print(adict1)
del adict1['two'] #this deletes the key-value pair whose key is 'two'
print(adict1)
```

This outputs

```
{'1': 'first', 'two': 'second', 'my3': '3rd'}
{'1': 'first', 'my3': '3rd'}
```

Searching Through a Dictionary

We want to search a dictionary to see if a specific key is contained in it. In this case, we want to see if 'a' and 'c' are keys in the dictionary.

In Python

```
>>> my_dict = {'a' : 'one', 'b' : 'two'}

>>> 'a' in my_dict
TRUE
>>> 'c' in my_dict
FALSE
```

The following code is held in the file adict5aa.py:

```
adict5aa.py
print("Enter key to be tested: ")
testkey = input()
my_dict = {'a' : 'one', 'b' : 'two'}
print (my_dict.get(testkey, "none"))
```

This outputs (if you enter "a" when asked for a key)

```
Enter key to be tested:
a
one
```

or outputs (if you enter "x" when asked for a key)

```
Enter key to be tested:
x
none
```

We have seen what dictionaries can do. We now look at tuples.

Tuples

A tuple contains items which are immutable. The elements of a tuple can be separated by commas within brackets or individual quoted elements separated by commas. They are accessed in a similar way to arrays, whereby the elements are numbered from 0. In this section, we will look at creating, concatenating, reading, deleting, and searching through tuples.

For example, define two tuples called firsttup and secondttup:

```
firsttup = ('a', 'b', 'c', 1, 2, 3)
secondtup = "a", "b", 10,  25
```

The following code refers to the third element of firsttup:

```
firsttup[2]
gives
c
```

The following code refers to the third element of firsttup:

```
firsttup[3]
gives
1
secondtup = "a", "b", 10,  25
```

The following code refers to the second element of secondtup:

```
secondtup[1]
gives
b
```

The following code refers to the third element of secondtup:

```
secondtup[2]
gives
10
```

We can also use negative indices to select from the end and work backward, for example,

```
secondtup[-1]
```

which gives

```
25
secondtup[-2]
```

which gives

```
10
```

Tuples cannot be amended.
So if we had

```
firsttup = ('a', 'b' 'c', 1, 2, 3)
firsttup[3] = 9
```

we would get

```
  File "<stdin>", line 1, in <module>

  TypeError: 'tuple' object does not support item assignment
```

Creating a Tuple

```
# An empty tuple
empty_tuple = ()
print (empty_tuple)
()

# Creating non-empty tuples

# One way of creation
tup = 'first', 'second'
```

```
print(tup)
('first', 'second')

# Another for doing the same
tup = ('first', 'second')
print(tup)
('first', 'second')
```

Concatenating Two Tuples

```
# Code for concatenating 2 tuples

tuple1 = (0, 1, 2, 3)
tuple2 = ('first', 'second')

# Concatenating above two
print(tuple1 + tuple2)
(0, 1, 2, 3, 'first', 'second')
```

Creating Nested Tuples

```
# Code for creating nested tuples

tuple1 = (0, 1, 2, 3)
tuple2 = ('first', 'second')
tuple3 = (tuple1, tuple2)
print(tuple3)
gives
((0, 1, 2, 3), ('first', 'second'))
```

Creating Repeated Tuples

```
# Code to create a tuple with repetition

tuple3 = ('first',)*3
print(tuple3)
gives
('first', 'first', 'first')
```

Converting a List or a String into a Tuple

```
# Code for converting a list and a string into a tuple

list1 = [0, 1, 2]
print(tuple(list1))
(0, 1, 2)
print(tuple('first')) # string 'first'
('f', 'i', 'r', 's', 't')
```

Creating Single-Element Tuple

```
# Creating tuple with single element (note that we still require the comma)
t=(1,)
print(t)
gives
(1,)
```

Reading Tuple

```
# Reading from start (index starts at zero)
tup1=(2,3,4,5,6,7)
tup[3]
gives
5
```

```
# Reading from  end (index starts at -1)
tup1[-1]
gives
7
```

Searching Within a Tuple

```
# Search
tup1=(2,3,4,5,6,7)
print (6 in tup1) # this tests if 6 is contained in tup1
gives
```

```
True
print (9 in tup1)
gives
False
```

Deleting a Tuple

```
# Deleting a complete Tuple
del tup1
print(tup1)
gives
```

```
    NameError: name 'tup1' is not defined
```

Using Tuple to Create Variables

```
# define our tuple as
aTuple = (10, 20, 30, 40)
# Now we can assign each of its elements to separate variables
a, b, c, d = aTuple
print(a)
gives
10
print(b)
gives
20
print(c)
gives
30
print(d)
gives
40
```

We have covered definitions and uses of different types of variables in this section. We will now look at the use of "if" statements.

If Then Else

When a decision has to be made in your program to either do one operation or the other, we use if statements.

These are fairly straightforward. Basically, we say

```
if (something is true)
        Perform a task
```

This is the basic form of if.

We can extend this to say

```
if (a condition  is true)
      Perform a task
else if it does not satisfy the above condition
        Perform a different task
```

Here is some Python code to demonstrate this:

```
number = 5
if number > 3:
   print('greater than 3')

number = 5
if number > 3:
   print('greater than 3')
else:
   print('not greater than 3')
```

Type in this code into a program and run it. It should come as no surprise that the output is

```
greater than 3
```

You could modify the program so that you input the number to be tested, but don't forget that for this code you need number = int(input ("Enter number :")) to enter a number.

This section has shown the importance of "if" statements in programming. Now we will look at loops.

Loops (For and While)

When we were doing many calculations in a program, it could be a bit of a chore to do a similar thing with, say, ten numbers. We could have done it by repeating similar code ten times. We can make this a bit simpler by writing one piece of code but then looping round the same piece of code ten times. This is called a "for loop." We will also look at "while" loops.

For Loops

Here is an example of how a for loop can help us.

The statement is

```
'for x in variable
    Carry out some code'
```

So if we have a variable as the following

forloopvar1 = [20, 13, 56, 9]

we can say

```
for x in forloopvar1: # go through forloop1 and place each element  in x
    print(x)  #this is the only instruction within the loop
```

outputs

```
20
13
56
9
```

The "range" instruction in Python has the general format

range(start, stop, step)

where

"start" is the start value of the index. Default is 0.

"stop" is 1 less than the last index to be used.

"step" is by how much the index is incremented. Default is 1.

Here is an example using the "range" instruction.

The program goes round the for loop starting with variables number and total set to 1.

Within the loop, it multiplies the current value of the number by the running total. Then it adds 1 to the number. So it is working out 1*2*3*4*5*6*7*8*9*10 or "10 factorial" (10!).

```
number = 1
total = 1
for x in range(10): ): #so here start is 0 (default), stop is 10-1, and
step is 1
        total = total * number
        number = number + 1
print(total)
```

This outputs

```
3628800
```

which you can check with your scientific calculator is 10 factorial.

```
for x in range(3, 6): # starts with 3 and ends with 6-1
    print(x)
```

This outputs

```
3
4
5
```

We can also have a list of values instead of a range, as shown in the next program.

This goes through the values and finds the index position of the value 46. We can see that 46 is in position 9 (counting from 0).

```
forloopvar1 = [20, 13, 56, 9, 32, 19, 87, 51, 70, 46, 56]
count = 0
for x in forloopvar1:
    if x == 46:
        break
        count = count + 1
print(count)
```

This outputs

```
9
```

While Loops

The logic of "while" loops is similar to our for loops.

Here, we say

```
'while x is true
     Carry out some code'
```

So we could have the following code which keeps adding 1 to count until count is no longer less than 10. Within the loop, the user is asked to enter integers. These are added to a total which is printed out at the end of the loop.

```
total = 0;
number = 0
# while loop goes round 10 times
while number < 10 :

    # ask the user to enter the integer number
    n = int(input('Enter a number: '))

    total = total + n
    number = number + 1
print('Total Sum is = ', total)
```

So if the user enters the number shown in the following, we get the total:

```
Enter a number: 1
Enter a number: 2
Enter a number: 3
Enter a number: 4
Enter a number: 5
Enter a number: 6
Enter a number: 7
Enter a number: 8
Enter a number: 9
Enter a number: 10
Total Sum is =  55
```

We have seen the importance of loops in this section. Our next section looks at switches.

Switches

In C programming, there is an instruction used widely called "switch." However, because there is no switch statement in Python, this section will demonstrate some code that can be included into your programs to perform the same function.

A switch jumps to a piece of code depending on the value of the variable it receives. For instance, if you had to perform different code for people in their 30s to that for people in their 40s and different to people in their 50s, we could have the following code. Here we have the value in "option" which determines which code we jump to.

The code for this function is in the file aswitch3.py:

```
aswitch3.py
def switch(option):
    if option == 30:
                print("Code for people in their 30s")
    elif option == 40:
                print("Code for people in their 40s")

    elif option == 50:

                print("Code for people in their 50s")

    else:
        print("Incorrect option")
#main code in the program where you enter 30,40 or 50 and the function
'switch' is called which uses the appropriate number as shown.
 optionentered = int(input("enter your option (30, 40 or 50 : ) "))
switch(optionentered)
running this program and entering '50' gives
enter your option : 50
Code for people in their 50s
```

This section has shown how to perform a switch in Python. We now move onto an important library of functions in Python. This is called "numpy."

Arithmetic Operations Using Numpy

Numpy is a library of mathematical functions that can be included into your Python program. It is useful in manipulating arrays, reading text files, and working with mathematical formulas. Numpy can be installed in various ways. One way is using "pip" from the command line as shown as follows:

```
pip install numpy
```

It is particularly useful in manipulating matrices (or arrays with extra dimensions). The arrays we have looked at so far are one-dimensional arrays. In this section, we will look at arrays with more dimensions. A one-dimensional array can also be called a "rank 1 array."

```
onedarray = array('i', [10,20,30,40,50])
```

We import numpy into our program using "import numpy", and we assign a link for our program. Here we define the link as "np" so the full line of code is

```
import numpy as np
```

The numpy function "shape" returns the dimensions of the array. So if your array was defined as

```
b = np.array([[1,2,3],[4,5,6]])
```

then the array would be a 2x3 matrix (two rows and three columns) as shown as follows:

```
[[1 2 3]
 [4 5 6]]
```

So if you now type

```
print(b.shape)
```

you would get

```
(2, 3)
```

as the shape.

The code for this function is in the file numpy1.py:

```
import numpy as np

a = np.array([1, 2, 3])      # Create a rank 1 array
print(type(a))               # Prints "<class 'numpy.ndarray'>"
print(a.shape)               # Prints "(3,)"
print(a[0], a[1], a[2])      # Prints "1 2 3"
a[0] = 5                     # Change an element of the array
print(a)                     # Prints "[5, 2, 3]"

b = np.array([[1,2,3],[4,5,6]])     # Create a rank 2 array


#1 2 3
#4 5 6
# reference elements counting from 0
# so b[1, 2] is row 1 (2nd row) column 2 (3rd column)
#so if you print b[1, 2] you get 6
print("b[1, 2] follows")
print(b[1, 2])

print(b.shape)                       # Prints "(2, 3)" 2 rows 3 columns
print(b[0, 0], b[0, 1], b[0, 2])     # Prints "1 2 3"
print(b[1, 0], b[1, 1], b[1, 2])     # Prints "4 5 6"
print(b[0, 0], b[0, 1], b[1, 0])     # Prints "1 2 4"
```

The normal mathematical representation of a matrix is as shown as follows:

$$\begin{pmatrix} 1 & 2 & 3 \\ 4 & 5 & 6 \end{pmatrix}$$

This is what we have defined in the preceding code using the following line of code:

```
b = np.array([[1,2,3],[4,5,6]])     # Create a rank 2 array
```

Matrix arithmetic can be understood by looking at real-life examples. The following are tables of three people working for a computer company. The first table shows how many laptops and how many printers each person sells in a month.

In Store Sale

Person	Laptops	Printers
Joe	4	5
Mary	6	7
Jen	7	9

The next table shows how many laptops and printers each person has sold online.

Online Sale

Person	Laptops	Printers
Joe	6	22
Mary	21	24
Jen	41	17

These tables can be represented by matrices as shown in the following. We add each term in the first matrix to the corresponding term in the second matrix to give the totals shown in the third matrix.

$$\begin{pmatrix} 4 & 5 \\ 6 & 7 \\ 7 & 9 \end{pmatrix} + \begin{pmatrix} 6 & 22 \\ 21 & 24 \\ 41 & 17 \end{pmatrix} = \begin{pmatrix} 10 & 27 \\ 27 & 31 \\ 48 & 26 \end{pmatrix}$$

The next table shows the total of laptops and printers sold by each person:

Total/Overall Sale

Person	Laptops	Printers
Joe	10	27
Mary	27	31
Jen	48	26

If each person doubles their total sales the following month, we can just multiply their current sales total by 2 as shown as follows:

$$2 \text{ X} \begin{pmatrix} 10 & 27 \\ 27 & 31 \\ 48 & 26 \end{pmatrix} = \begin{pmatrix} 20 & 54 \\ 54 & 62 \\ 96 & 52 \end{pmatrix}$$

We now look at their totals for the first month and have another table containing the cost of a laptop and the cost of a printer.

Total Sales

Person	Laptops	Printers		Cost/Item list with cost	
Joe	10	27		Laptop	200
Mary	27	31		Printer	25
Jen	48	26			

We can work out how much money each person makes for the company my multiplying their total number of sales of a laptop by its cost. Then we multiply their total number of sales of printers by its cost and then add these two together. The table and the corresponding matrix representations of this are shown as follows:

	Sales Cost
Joe	10x200 + 27x25 = 2975
Mary	27x200 + 31x25 = 3875
Jen	48x200 + 26x25 = 4775

There is a rule when multiplying matrices. The number of columns in the first matrix has to be equal to the number of rows of the second matrix.

So if we say that a matrix is 2x3 (two rows and three columns), then it can multiply a 3x2 or a 3x3 or a 3.4, etc. matrix. It cannot multiply a 2x3 or 2x4 or 4x2 or 4x3, etc.

$$\begin{pmatrix} 10 & 27 \\ 27 & 31 \\ 48 & 26 \end{pmatrix} \times \begin{pmatrix} 200 \\ 25 \end{pmatrix} = \begin{pmatrix} 10\text{x}200 + 27\text{x}25 \\ 27\text{x}200 + 31\text{x}25 \\ 48\text{x}200 + 26\text{x}25 \end{pmatrix} =$$

$$\begin{pmatrix} 2975 \\ 3875 \\ 4775 \end{pmatrix}$$

In the multiplication in the preceding diagram, we see it is (3x2) x (2x1) producing a (3x1) matrix.

Numpy Calculations

Listings 1-1 through 1-5 are some programs to show basic numpy calculations with matrices.

Add two 2x2 matrices.

Listing 1-1. numpmat.py

```python
import numpy as np

a = np.array(([3,1],[6,4]))

b = np.array(([1,8],[4,2]))

c = a + b

print('matrix a is')
print(a)
print('matrix b is')
print(b)
print('matrix c is')
print(c)
```

This outputs

```
matrix a is
[[3 1]
 [6 4]]
matrix b is
[[1 8]
 [4 2]]
matrix c is
[[ 4  9]
 [10  6]]
```

Add a 2x3 matrix to another 2x3 matrix.

Listing 1-2. numpmat2.py

```python
import numpy as np

a = np.array(([1,2,3],[4,5,6]))

b = np.array(([3,2,1],[6,5,4]))

d = a + b

c = 2*a

print('matrix a is')
print(a)
print('matrix b is')
print(b)
print('matrix d is')
print(d)
print('matrix c is')
print(c)
```

This outputs

```
matrix a is
[[1 2 3]
 [4 5 6]]
matrix b is
[[3 2 1]
 [6 5 4]]
matrix d is
[[ 4  4  4]
 [10 10 10]]
matrix c is
[[ 2  4  6]
 [ 8 10 12]]
```

Add a 2x2 matrix to a 2x2 matrix both floating point.

Listing 1-3. numpmat3.py

```python
import numpy as np

a = np.array(([3.1,1.2],[6.3,4.5]))

b = np.array(([1.3,8.6],[4.9,2.8]))

c = a + b

print('matrix a is')
print(a)
print('matrix b is')
print(b)
print('matrix c is')
print(c)
```

This outputs

```
matrix a is
[[3.1 1.2]
 [6.3 4.5]]
matrix b is
[[1.3 8.6]
 [4.9 2.8]]
matrix c is
[[ 4.4  9.8]
 [11.2  7.3]]
```

Multiply a 3x2 matrix by a 2x1 matrix.

Listing 1-4. numpmat4.py

```python
import numpy as np

a = np.array(([1,2],[4,5],[6,8]))

b = np.array(([3],[6]))

c = np.matmul(a,b) #matmul is the numpy function for multiplying matrices
```

```
print('matrix a is')
print(a)
print('matrix b is')
print(b)
print('matrix c is')
print(c)
```

This outputs

```
matrix a is
[[1 2]
 [4 5]
 [6 8]]
matrix b is
[[3]
 [6]]
matrix c is
[[15]
 [42]
 [66]]
```

Multiply a 3x2 matrix by a 2x3 matrix.

If you did this manually with pen and paper, this is how you would do it:

$$\begin{pmatrix} 1 & 2 \\ 3 & 4 \\ 5 & 6 \end{pmatrix} \times \begin{pmatrix} 7 & 8 & 9 \\ 10 & 11 & 12 \end{pmatrix} =$$

$$\begin{pmatrix} 1x7 + 2x10 & 1x8 + 2x11 & 1x9 + 2x12 \\ 3x7 + 4x10 & 3x8 + 4x11 & 3x9 + 4x12 \\ 5x7 + 6x10 & 5x8 + 6x11 & 5x9 + 6x12 \end{pmatrix} = \begin{pmatrix} 27 & 30 & 33 \\ 61 & 68 & 75 \\ 95 & 106 & 117 \end{pmatrix}$$

Note the way you do the multiplication by hand, 1st row x 1st column, 1st row x 2nd column, 1st row x 3rd column, then 2nd row, and then 3rd row. Of course, if you use numpy's matmul function, it is all done for you.

Listing 1-5. *numpmat5.py*

```python
import numpy as np

a = np.array(([1,2],[3,4],[5,6]))

b = np.array(([7,8,9],[10,11,12]))

c = np.matmul(a,b)

print('matrix a is')
print(a)
print('matrix b is')
print(b)
print('matrix c is')
print(c)
```

This outputs

```
matrix a is
[[1 2]
 [3 4]
 [5 6]]
matrix b is
[[ 7  8  9]
 [10 11 12]]
matrix c is
[[ 27  30  33]
 [ 61  68  75]
 [ 95 106 117]]
```

This section has explored the important numpy mathematical functions in Python.

Mathematical Graph Functions

In a similar way that we included the numpy library into our programs, we can include graph plotting libraries called "matplotlib.pyplot" so we can access the graph functions library with the code

```python
import matplotlib.pyplot as plt
```

In our program, this makes plt our pointer to matplotlib.pyplot.

You can install matplotlib using the "pip" instruction

```
pip install matplotlib
```

The program here is going to plot a graph of the marks that people got in an examination.

The code for this function is in the file mp1a.py:

```
mp1a.py
import matplotlib.pyplot as plt
# x values:
marks = list(range(0, 100, 10)) #marks (x values) divided into equal values
up to 100
print(marks) # write the values calculated by the previous instruction
```

This produces

```
[0, 10, 20, 30, 40, 50, 60, 70, 80, 90]
 # y values:
people = [4, 7, 9, 17, 22, 25, 28, 18, 6, 2]
# label the axes
plt.xlabel('marks')
plt.ylabel('people')
plt.plot(marks, people)
plt.show()
```

and outputs

```
[0, 10, 20, 30, 40, 50, 60, 70, 80, 90]
```

These plot the graph shown in Figure 1-1.

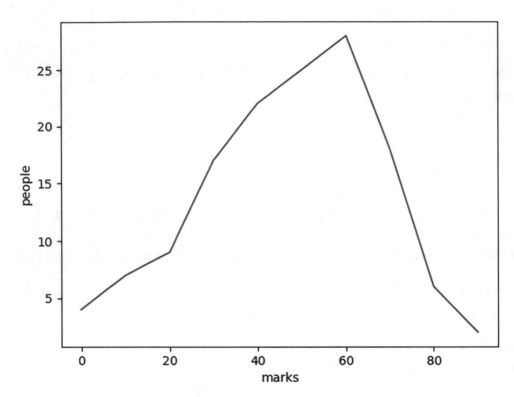

Figure 1-1. *Example of plotting (x,y) points*

We see from the graph that most people got marks between about 30 and 70, which is what you would expect. A few got low marks and only a few got high marks.

The next program, mp2aa.py, plots two graphs on the same axes. Here we plot examination marks gained by females and those gained by males. We plot females as one color and males as another.

The code for this function is in the file mp2aa.py:

```
mp2aa.py
import matplotlib.pyplot as plt
# x values:
marks = list(range(0,100,10)) #marks (x values) divided into equal values
up to 100
# y values (number of students whose marks lie within each x range):
male = [4, 7, 9, 17, 22, 25, 28, 18, 6, 2]
female = [2, 5, 8, 13, 28, 25, 23, 20, 18, 12]
```

```
plt.xlabel('marks')
plt.ylabel('number of students')

plt.title('Comparison of male / female examination scores')
#plot the female graph
plt.plot(marks, female, label="female")
plt.plot(marks, female, "ob")
#plot the male graph
plt.plot(marks, male, label="male")
plt.plot(marks, male, "or")

plt.legend()
plt.show()
```

This produces the following graph shown in Figure 1-2.

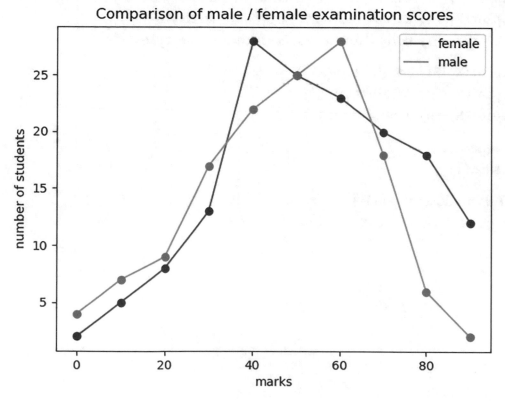

Figure 1-2. *Example of plotting two graphs*

The next program, ml1pj.py, plots three graphs on the same axes. Here, we plot y = sin(x), y = 2sin(x), and y = cos(x). We plot each one in a different color.

This demonstrates some of the mathematical functions available to matplotlib.

The code for this function is in the file ml1pj.py:

```
ml1pj.py
import matplotlib.pyplot as plt
import numpy as np
X = np.linspace(0, 2 * np.pi, 50, endpoint=True) # set x values as
multiples of pi

F1 = 2 * np.sin(X) # y = 2sin(x)
F2 = np.sin(X) #y = sin(x)
F3 = np.cos(X) #y = cos(x)

plt.plot(X, F1, color="blue", linewidth=2, linestyle="-")
plt.plot(X, F2, color="red", linewidth=2, linestyle="-")
plt.plot(X, F3, color="green", linewidth=2, linestyle="-")

plt.plot(X, F1, label="2sin(x)")
plt.plot(X, F2, label="sin(x)")
plt.plot(X, F3, label="cos(x)")

plt.legend()
plt.show()
```

This produces Figure 1-3.

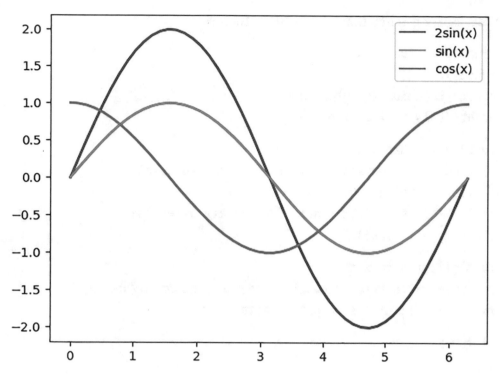

Figure 1-3. *Plotting three graphs*

This section has shown the importance of matplotlib in Python.

User-Written Functions

As well as having functions defined for you (like in numpy or Matlab), you can define functions for yourself.

A function is of the following format

```
def funcname(arguments)
```

where funcname is whatever you want to call your function and the parameters are information you need to pass to your function. The actual contents of the parameters will probably be different for different calls of the function.

If you want to return a value to the caller of the function, you can do this using the return command.

The code for this function is in the file tst16b.py:

```python
# Define our 3 functions
def func1():
    #basic function to output a string
    print("This is from func1")

def func2(name, pretax):
    # calculates a person's salary after tax is taken
    aftertax = pretax * 0.85
    print("%s This is from func1, Your salary after tax is
    %f"%(name,aftertax))

def func3(first,second,third):
    # simple arithmetic calculation on the 3 numbers submitted
    return 3.5*first + second/2 - third

# call func1
func1()

#call func2
func2("Bernard", 23.78)

#call func3
x = func3(1,2,3)
print(x)
```

This outputs

```
This is from func1
Bernard This is from func1, Your salary after tax is 20.213000
1.5
```

In reality, the functions you will define in your programs will be more complicated than those earlier as it would be just as easy, in the preceding cases, to write the code itself in the main body of your program as to call the function.

File Access

In Python programs, we can create, read from, write to, update, and delete files.

We will use the graph plotting functions from matplotlib as described in the section "Mathematical Graph Functions." Again, to use matplotlib in a Python program, we need the following line of code at the start of the program.

The following program, re11pjc.py, reads the pjfiley.txt file, which contains the following 11 lines of data:

```
#pjfiley.txt
a#This is my linexxxxxxxxxxxxxx
b#second linexxxx
c#third linexx
d#fourth linexxxxxxxxxxxxxxxxxxxxxxxxxxxxxxxxxxxxxxxxxxxxxxxxxxxxxxxxx
e#fifth line
f#sixth
g#seventh
h#eighth
i#nineth
j#tenth
k#eleventh
```

The program opens the file and stores a pointer to it in "fhand". It then performs a for loop which reads each line from the file and stores the current line in "line". The object of the program is to find the line with the character "k" at the start of the line. When it finds this, it prints out the rest of the line. It uses the function "line.split" to split the line when it comes across the "#" character. Then, the "k" is stored in "a", and the rest of the line is stored in "b".

```
#re11pjc.py
fhand = open('pjfiley.txt')
# read each line from the file
for line in fhand:
    if line[0]=='k': # is the first character of the current line 'k'
        a,b = line.split('#') # split the line into two parts, separated by
        the '#' in the line
        print(b)
```

```
fhand.close()
```

this prints
eleventh

As the line starting with k is k#eleventh, when we split this between either side of the #, we store the "k" in the storage location "a" and "eleventh" in storage location "b".

The following program reads the Peoplex.txt file, which contains the following:

```
#Peoplex
a-Jones-37-accountant

b-Smith-42-HR

c-Allen-28-Secretary

d-Bradley-26-Programmer

e-Edwards-41-Programmer

f-King-35-S/W engineer

g-Price-39-H/W engineer

h-Roberts-52-Manager

i-Foster-44-Analyst

j-Shannon-24-Programmer

k-Lewis-27-Receptionist
```

This is a data file containing information about workers in a company. Each line is used for one worker. The first character in the line is a reference character which uniquely identifies the worker. The other fields in the line identify their name, their age, and their job title. Each field is separated by the "-" character, which we use to separate the fields using the line.split() function.

The following program reads through the file to find the worker with ID specified by the user. When the program finds it, it splits the line into separate fields. We can print out this data by concatenating these fields.

```
#re11pjd.py
fhand = open('Peoplex.txt')

# user is asked to enter the ID character of the line they wish to read.
n = input('Enter an ID: ')

for line in fhand:
   if line[0]==n:
      a,b,c,d = line.split('-') # specified line is found so split it into
      4 components
      print(b+' '+c+' '+d) # concatenate the 2nd, 3rd and 4th components

fhand.close()
```

If we enter "d", we get the output

```
Enter an ID: d
Bradley 26 Programmer
Amend a field in one of the lines
```

The file pjfilezi.bin contains the following data:

```
a-Jones-37-accountant
b-Smith-33-welder
c-Allen-28-Secretary
d-Bradley-26-Programmer
```

We want to amend the age and job description of one of the entries.

The following code does this. We want to use one method of performing updates to a file. This method reads the file and writes each line to another file. When this has been completed, it copies the new file into the original file.

```
#re11pjdga.py
finphand = open('pjfilezi.bin','r') # input file
fouthand = open('pjfilezo.bin','w') # output file
#ask the user to enter the ID for the row to be amended.
n = input('Enter an ID: ')
#We want to update the age and job description to the following values.
age = input('Enter age: ')
desc = input('Enter job description: ')
```

```python
# find the correct line from the ID entered
for line in finphand:
    if line[0]==n:
         # we have found the correct line
        a,b,c,d = line.split('-') # split the line into its 4 components.
        print(a) #ID
        print(b) #name
        print(c) #age
        print(d) #occupation
        print(b+' '+c+' '+d) #concatenate and print the 2nd, 3rd and 4th
# update
        c=age
        d=desc
        print(b+' '+c+' '+d) # print the amended line
        line=(a+'-'+b+'-'+c+'-'+d+'\n') # store the amended line
        fouthand.write(line) # write the line to the output file

    else:
       # not found the line to be amended so write this line to the output
         file
        fouthand.write(line)

fouthand.close()
finphand.close()

#close and reopen the files and copy the output file to the input file
file1 = open("pjfilezo.bin", "r")
file2 = open("pjfilezi.bin", "w")
l = file1.readline()
while l:
    file2.write(l)
    l = file1.readline()
file1.close()
file2.close()
```

If we run the program and enter "c" as the ID and then change the age to 32 and job description to welder, we get

```
Enter an ID: c
Enter age: 32
Enter job description: welder
c
Allen
28
Secretary

Allen 28 Secretary

Allen 32 welder
```

The following program reads data from a file and uses it to plot a graph using matplotlib.

Various storage locations are printed at different stages of the program so that the user can monitor what the program is doing. These are shown after the graph plot. The following program reads the following from the output.txt file:

```
2.4*x+7.9
0, 20
```

The first line is the equation to be plotted $(y = 2.4 * x + 7.9)$.

The second line is the range of x values to use in the plot.

```
# readfilec2.py###################
```

The program reads the two lines:

```
import matplotlib.pyplot as plt
import numpy as np

fhand = open('output.txt','r')
lines = [' ',' ']
count = 0
#store the two lines in lines[0] and lines[1]
```

```
for line in fhand:
    lines[count] = line
    count = count + 1
print('lines[0] The first line read from output.txt')
print(lines[0])
print('lines[1] The second line read from output.txt')
print(lines[1])
#strip the newline character from each of the lines
l1 = lines[0].rstrip('\n')
l2 = lines[1].rstrip('\n')
print('l1 The first line read from output.txt with newline character
removed ')
print(l1)
print('l2 The second line read from output.txt with newline character
removed ')
print(l2)
```

Import matplot lib is required only when we use this function, try to put the above blocks of code in different modules and import all into another file and plot

```
def graph(formula, x_range):
# function to plot the graph
    x = np.array(x_range)
    y = eval(formula) # evaluate the formula to give the y-values
    plt.xlabel('x values')
    plt.ylabel('y values')
    plt.title('Line Graph ')
    plt.plot(x, y)
    plt.show()
#get the second line and store the two points on aint and bint
aint=int(l2[3])
#b = 0
bint=int(l2[0])
# call the graph-plotting function with the equation and range as
parameters
graph(l1, range(bint, aint))
```

The program produces the graph shown in Figure 1-4.

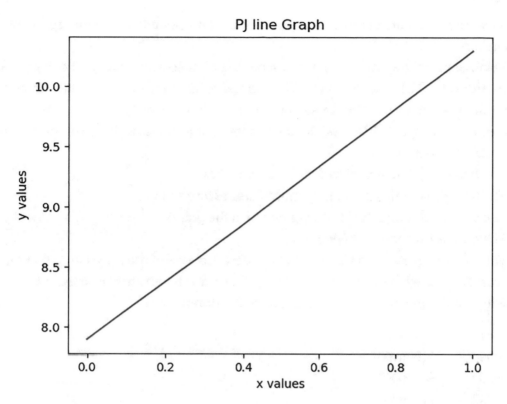

Figure 1-4. *Plot of y = 2.4x + 7.9*

This program outputs the following:

```
lines[0] The first line read from output.txt
2.4*x+7.9

lines[1] The second line read from output.txt
0, 20

l1 The first line read from output.txt with newline character removed
2.4*x+7.9
l2 The second line read from output.txt with newline character removed
0, 20
```

Regressions

The next program plots a line of regression and the four points used in the regression calculation.

Regression is the approximation of a series of points to a straight line. So here, the points are (1,2), (2,5), (3,6), and (4,9). The regression line for these points has already been calculated as y = 0 + 2.2x. This information has been stored into three files, which are read by the program. The straight line and the four points are plotted onto a graph to illustrate the regression.

The following program takes data from three files.

The first file contains the x and y coordinates of four points.

The second contains the line of regression of the points.

The third is the number of points.

Various storage locations are printed at different stages of the program so that the user can monitor what the program is doing. These are shown after the graph plot.

Files read by the following program and their contents:

```
capm.bin
1.000000      2.000000
2.000000      5.000000
3.000000      6.000000
4.000000      9.000000

capm2.bin
0.000000+2.200000*x

capm2cnt.bin
4
```

The program uses two methods of accessing files:

```
fhand = open('capm2.bin','r')
```

and

```
z = np.loadtxt("capm2cnt.bin")
#readfile7a2.py
import matplotlib.pyplot as plt
import numpy as np
```

```
fhand = open('capm2.bin','r') #file containing the calculated regression
equation
# 'capm.bin' is the file containing the coordinate points
# 'capm2cnt.bin' is the # file containing the number of coordinate points

z = np.loadtxt("capm2cnt.bin") # read the number of points and store in z
print("Data read from capm2cnt.bin")
print("z follows")
print(z)
a = z # this is the number of coordinate points
zint = int(a) # convert the number to an int
print("zint follows")
print(zint)
count = 0
y = np.loadtxt("capm.bin") # read the 4 points and store in y
print("Data read from capm.bin")
print(y)
# y now contains the x and y values of the 4 points
#[[1. 2.]
# [2. 5.]
# [3. 6.]
# [4. 9.]]

#zeroise the two arrays using zint as the count of points
xvals = [0]*zint
yvals = [0]*zint

print("xvalsfirst")
print(xvals)
print("yvalsfirst")
print(yvals)
#separate the x and y values
for x in range(zint):
    a,b = y[x]
    xvals[x] = a
    yvals[x] = b
```

```
print("xvals")
print(xvals)
print("yvals")
print(yvals)

plt.plot(xvals, yvals, "ob")
# read the calculated regression equation from 'capm2.bin' (pointed to by
fhand)
count = 0
for line in fhand:
    line = line.rstrip() #rstrip() strips space characters from end of
string
print(line) # the calculated regression equation

# set the x values for the graph
x = np.linspace(-5,5,10)
print('x follows')
print(x)
print('line follows')
print(line)
#line is 0.000000+2.200000*x

a = 'y='
b = a + line # b is y = 0.000000+2.200000*x

print(b)
# line contains the regression equation
# The eval command carries out the function contained in 'line'. In this
case it is 'y = 0.0 + 2.2*x'
# It takes the values of x from the x = np.linspace(-5,5,10) code above and
calculates y values.
y= eval(line) # use the regression equation to calculate the y-values from
the x-values above
print('y follows')
print(y)

plt.plot(x, y, '-r', label=b)
#Plot the regression line and the four points
```

```
plt.title(b)
plt.xlabel('x', color='#1C2833')
plt.ylabel('y', color='#1C2833')
plt.legend(loc='upper left')
plt.grid()
plt.show()
```

The program produces the graph shown in Figure 1-5.

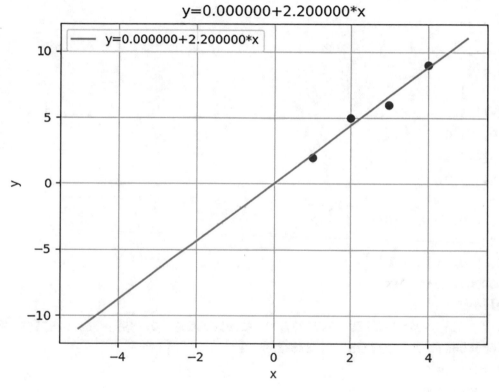

Figure 1-5. *Plot of y = 0.0 + 2.2x*

You can see from the graph that all of the points are close to the line. Rather than just say that the points are close to the line, fairly close to the line, or not very close to the line, we can use a number which tells us how close to the line the points are. This number has a name. It is called the "Product Moment Correlation Coefficient," usually abbreviated to PMCC. In the preceding case, if the points were on the line, the PMCC would be 1. As they are close to the line, the PMCC would be something like 0.92145. We will look at PMCC later in the book.

The output from this program is as follows:

```
Data read from capm2cnt.bin

z follows
4.0
zint follows
4

Data read from capm.bin

[[1. 2.]
 [2. 5.]
 [3. 6.]
 [4. 9.]]
xvalsfirst
[0, 0, 0, 0]
yvalsfirst
[0, 0, 0, 0]
xvals
[1.0, 2.0, 3.0, 4.0]
yvals
[2.0, 5.0, 6.0, 9.0]
0.000000+2.200000*x
x follows
[-5.         -3.88888889 -2.77777778 -1.66666667 -0.55555556  0.55555556
  1.66666667  2.77777778  3.88888889  5.         ]
line follows
0.000000+2.200000*x
y=0.000000+2.200000*x
y follows
[-11.          -8.55555556  -6.11111111  -3.66666667  -1.22222222
   1.22222222   3.66666667   6.11111111   8.55555556  11.          ]
```

This section has explored file handling in Python.

Summary

This chapter demonstrates the fundamentals of Python programming. It shows the different data types, how they are defined and their properties, the numpy and matplotlib links that perform mathematical and graphical functions, and file handling.

The next chapter will explore the fundamentals and uses of C code.

Exercises

1. Perform the same arithmetic operations we used for our int values as in the example in section 1.1.1

   using
   V1 = 2
   V2 = 3.5
   V3 = 5.1
   V4 = 6.75

2. From section 1.1.3

   Create a list of numbers starting from 1 to 7. Print this list, and then append the next seven numbers that is 8 to 14 to the list using a for loop (see section "For Loops").

   Create a dictionary with elements {'a' : \one\, 'b' :"two'}. Ask the user to enter a key to be tested. Test if the key is in your dictionary using a for loop (see section "For Loops"). Output an appropriate message to say whether you find it or not.

   Create a tuple with elements even numbers from 2 to 14. Print out the elements using a for loop (see section "For Loops").

3. From section 1.1.10

   Amend the file workers' data file program to create a file which also has their initial after their name and to add their salary at the end of the line.

CHAPTER 2

C Programming

In this chapter, we'll review the C programming language. If you don't already have a C development environment on your computer, you can download it, free of charge, from Microsoft. You can download their Microsoft Development Kit (SDK). Another way you can access C is by using Visual Studio. Again, a version of this can be downloaded.

C Program Format

Listing 2-1 is a simple C program which asks the user to enter a character, reads the character, and then prints it to the screen. We will use this to show the basic format of a C program.

It is helpful, when you have written a lot of programs, to give each program a relevant title. This program is called c1.2readprint.c, "c1.2," because it is in the first part of Chapter 2 and "readprint" because it reads and prints a character. The ".c" at the end of the program name is essential for any C program. C programs will not compile if they do not have this. The compiler converts your program into machine code which the hardware in the computer understands.

In the following program, int main() delimits your code between the { and the } (although we will see later that you can write a separate piece of code outside of the main() part and call it from the main() part. The #include<stdio.h> is a command to tell the compiler to attach to your executable program the code which executes the getchar() and putchar(). stdio refers to the standard input and output library.

Comments are written in this program that show/remind what is being done in the program. They are written between /* and */. As shown here, they can be written after the C code on the same line or on separate lines.

© Philip Joyce 2022
P. Joyce, *C and Python Applications*, https://doi.org/10.1007/978-1-4842-7774-4_2

The "printf" in the code tells the computer to print whatever is between each of the double quotes.

The getchar and putchar instructions read and print a character.

Listing 2-1. c1.2readprint.c

```
#include <stdio.h>
/* read and display a number */
int main () {
   char c; /* store area where the character read in will be kept */

   printf("Enter character: "); /* ask the user to enter a character */
   c = getchar(); /* read the character in */

   printf("Character entered: "); /* tell the user what character the
   program has read */
   putchar(c); /* write the character */

   return(0);
}
```

The char c; instruction means that you are reserving a place in your program where you will store the character which is read in. c can then be referred to as a "variable" in your program. In the code c=getchar(), the = sign means "assign to." So the instruction is saying get the character and assign it to the variable c. Type in a character. Your program should reply with the character you typed in. Now type your first name. What happens? getchar() only reads one character, and it will only store the first character you typed into the char c data store in your program. Note the comments in the program telling you what is going on. I

Adding Two Numbers

In Listing 2-2, we ask the user to enter two integers. Then we add these and print the answer. Then we ask the user to enter two float numbers, and we add these and display the answer.

Listing 2-2. c1.2addtwodf.c

```c
#define _CRT_SECURE_NO_WARNINGS
#include<stdio.h>

int main()
{
        int int_number1, int_number2, itotal; /* storage areas for the int
        numbers */
        float float_number1, float_number2, ftotal; /* storage areas for the
        float numbers */

        /* ask the user to enter two integers */

        printf("Please enter an integer number:\n ");
        scanf("%d", &int_number1); /* read integer number in */
        printf("You entered %d\n", int_number1);

        printf("Please enter another integer number: \n");
        scanf("%d", &int_number2); /* read integer number in */
        printf("You entered %d\n", int_number2);

        /* add the two numbers into 'total' and display the answer */

        itotal = int_number1 + int_number2; /* add two numbers */
        printf("total is %d\n", itotal);

        /* ask the user to enter two floating point (decimal) numbers */

        printf("Please enter a float number:\n ");
        scanf("%f", &float_number1); /* read decimal number in */
        printf("You entered %f\n", float_number1);

        printf("Please enter another float number: \n");
        scanf("%f", &float_number2); /* read decimal number in */
        printf("You entered %f\n", float_number2);

        /* add the two numbers into 'total' and display the answer */
```

```
    ftotal = float_number1 + float_number2; /* add the numbers */
    printf("total is %f\n", ftotal);

    return 0;
}
```

In this program, we are reading in integer and float numbers. We define the storage for each of our integer numbers using int as shown at the start of the program and float for the floating point numbers. We have also specified storage for where we want to store the total when we have added our numbers. This is itotal for the integers and ftotal for the float numbers. Notice that we can list all our storage names next to each other after the int command, as long as they are all int types. "Types" are the way we differentiate between our data, for example, whole numbers are "integer" or "int" and characters ,like "A", "$", and "?" are "char" types.

In this program, we use scanf to read the characters from the screen rather than getchar(). This is because our numbers to be added can be more than one character. The %d in scanf and printf specifies an integer to be read or written. The %f in scanf and printf specifies an integer to be read or written. In printf here, the answer to be printed is stored in itotal or ftotal.

Multiply and Divide Two Numbers

In Listing 2-3, we enter two floating point numbers. Firstly, we multiply them together and print the answer; then we divide the first number by the second and display the answer.

Listing 2-3. c1.2multdiv.c

```
#define _CRT_SECURE_NO_WARNINGS
#include <stdio.h>

/*  multiply two floating point numbers */

int main()
{
    float this_is_a_number1, this_is_a_number2, total; /* storage areas
    for the numbers */
```

```
/* ask the user to enter two floating point (decimal) numbers */

printf("Please enter a number:\n ");
scanf("%f", &this_is_a_number1); /* read number in */
printf("You entered %f\n", this_is_a_number1);

printf("Please enter another number: \n");
scanf("%f", &this_is_a_number2); /* read number in */
printf("You entered %f\n", this_is_a_number2);

 /* multiply  the two numbers into 'total' and display the answer */

total = this_is_a_number1 * this_is_a_number2; /* multiply the
numbers */
printf("product is %f\n", total);

/* divide  the two numbers into 'total' and display the answer */

total = this_is_a_number1 / this_is_a_number2; /* divide the numbers */
printf("quotient is %f\n", total);

return 0;
}
```

This section was concerned with basic data and arithmetic manipulation. The next section looks at the usefulness of using loops in programming.

For Loops

When we were doing our two numbers program, it would have been a bit of a chore to do a similar thing with, say, ten numbers. We could have done it by repeating similar code ten times. We can make this a bit simpler by writing one piece of code but then looping round the same piece of code ten times. This is called a "for loop."

Listing 2-4 is an example of how a for loop can help us.

Listing 2-4. c1.2for.c

```c
#define _CRT_SECURE_NO_WARNINGS
#include<stdio.h>
/* demonstrate a forloop */
main()

{
    float this_is_a_number, total; /* storage areas for the numbers */
    int i;

    total = 0;

    /* forloop goes round 10 times */
    for (i = 0;i < 10;i++)
    {
        /* ask the user to enter the floating point (decimal) number */

        printf("Please enter a number:\n ");
        scanf("%f", &this_is_a_number); /* read number in */
        total = total + this_is_a_number;

    }
    printf("Total Sum is = %f\n", total);
}
```

The syntax of the for statement is

for(initial value; final value; increment)

The code to go round the loop is contained with the { after the for statement and the } after the statements.

Within the for statement, the variable i is used as the variable to be incremented and tested while going through the loop. Its initial value of i is 0 as shown in the first part of the for statement; then each time the code is completed within the loop, 1 gets added to i (this is what i++ does). After each loop, a test is made to see if the i value has reached 10 (this is the i<10 part). When it does, the loop stops. So in this case, the code in the loop is executed ten times. Within the code, the user is asked to enter a number. This gets added into total in each loop, and then the final value is printed out.

Do While Loops

There is another method of doing a similar thing to a for loop, but it is formatted slightly differently. The loop says "do" – then within {}, again, contains a series of commands, ending with "while …" where the "…" is just a condition to be true. When the condition is not true, it drops out of the loop. So using a "do" loop to do the same thing as our for loop would be. The i++ instruction in the do loop just adds 1 to whatever i currently contains. To subtract 1, it's just i--.

```
#define _CRT_SECURE_NO_WARNINGS
#include<stdio.h>
/* demonstrate a do loop */
main()

{

    float this_is_a_number, total; /* storage areas for the numbers */
    int i;

    total = 0;
    i = 0;
    /* do loop goes round until the value of i reaches 10 */
    do {

        printf("Please enter a number:\n ");
        scanf("%f", &this_is_a_number);
        total = total + this_is_a_number;
        i++;

    }while( i < 10);
    printf("Total Sum is = %f\n", total);
}
```

You should find that you get the same result as your for loop program.

Having seen how useful loops can be we will now look at switches.

Switch Instruction

Another instruction that is useful in C is switch. This takes a value and jumps to an appropriate position in the code depending on the value. In Listing 2-5, the user can enter any integer value between 1 and 5.

The switch instruction takes the value, and if it is 1, it jumps to case 1:; if it is 2, it jumps to case 2:; and so on. If the number entered is not an integer from 1 to 5, it drops to the default: case where it outputs an error message.

Listing 2-5. c1.2swi.c

```c
#define _CRT_SECURE_NO_WARNINGS
#include <stdio.h>
/* Example of a switch operation */
int main()
{
    int this_is_a_number; /* storage areas for the numbers */

    /* ask the user to enter integer number */

    printf("Please enter an integer between 1 and 5:\n ");
    scanf("%d", &this_is_a_number);

    /* Move to the appropriate case statement corresponding to the
    entered number */

    switch (this_is_a_number)
    {

    case 1:
        printf("Case1: Value is: %d", this_is_a_number);
        break;
    case 2:
        printf("Case2: Value is: %d", this_is_a_number);
        break;
    case 3:
        printf("Case3: Value is: %d", this_is_a_number);
        break;
```

```
case 4:
        printf("Case4: Value is: %d", this_is_a_number);
        break;
case 5:
        printf("Case5: Value is: %d", this_is_a_number);
        break;
default:
        printf("Error Value is: %d", this_is_a_number); /* The number
        entered was not between 1 and 5 so report the error*/
}
return 0;
}
```

You can do a similar thing but using specific characters rather than numbers. You then jump to the appropriate place using the character as the case name, for example, if you type in a, then you jump to case a:.

The last section showed how you can use a switch statement to jump to a specific piece of code. The next section does a similar thing but uses "if" and "else" instead.

If Else

When a decision has to be made in your program to either do one operation or the other, we use if statements.

These are fairly straightforward. Basically, we say (the following is not actual code)

```
if (something is true)
    Perform a task
```

This is the basic form of if.
We can extend this to say

```
if (something is true)
    Perform a task
else
    Perform a different task
```

Here is some C code to demonstrate this:

```c
#include <stdio.h>
/* Example of an if operation */
int main()
{
    int this_is_a_number; /* storage area for the number*/
     /* ask the user to enter a specific integer */

    printf( "Please enter an integer between 1 and 10:\n " );
    scanf( "%d", &this_is_a_number );

    if (this_is_a_number <6)
        printf( "This number is less than 6;\n " );

    /* ask the user to enter another specific integer */

    printf( "Please enter an integer between 10 and 20:\n " );
    scanf( "%d", &this_is_a_number );

    if (this_is_a_number <16)
        printf( "This number is less than 16\n " );
    else
        printf( "This number is greater than 15\n " );

    return 0;
}
```

Create and test your program. When you are testing, it is good practice to test to each limit and to even enter incorrect data. Here there is no check to see if you really do enter within the ranges specified. You could add a test yourself.

There is an extension of the "if then else" type of command. This is the "if then else if" where you add an extra level of ifs. The following is an extension of your last program to add this.

If Else If

Listing 2-6 does the same if as the previous one, but instead of just an else following it, it does else if to test another option.

Listing 2-6. c1.2if.c

```c
#define _CRT_SECURE_NO_WARNINGS
#include <stdio.h>
/* Example of an if then else if operation */
int main()
{
    int this_is_a_number; /* storage area for the number*/

    /* ask the user to enter a specific integer */

    printf("Please enter an integer between 1 and 10:\n ");
    scanf("%d", &this_is_a_number);

    if (this_is_a_number < 6)
        printf("This number is less than 6;\n ");

    /* ask the user to enter another specific integer */

    printf("Please enter an integer between 10 and 20:\n ");
    scanf("%d", &this_is_a_number);

    if (this_is_a_number < 16)
    {
        printf("This number is less than 16\n ");
    }
    else if (this_is_a_number == 20)
    {
        printf("This number is 20\n ");
    }
    else
    {
        printf("This number is greater than 15\n ");
    }

    return 0;
}
```

So here, it tests if the number entered was less than 16. If it was, it prints "This number is less than 16"; otherwise, it then tests if the number equals 20. If it is, it prints out "This number is 20". Otherwise, it prints out "This number is greater than 15 but not 20".

Having seen the usefulness of "if" statements, we will now move to arrays.

Data Arrays

There is another way of storing data in our programs rather than in just individual locations. These are called "arrays." They can be defined as "int" where all the elements of the array are integers. They can be "char" where all the elements are character. There are also other types which we will see later. We define an integer array with the length of the array which we insert in square brackets, for example, int arr[8] for an array of eight elements. In this case, "arr" is the name of the array.

Listing 2-7 shows us how to read in eight integers and store them in an array.

Listing 2-7. c1.2arr.c

```
#define _CRT_SECURE_NO_WARNINGS
#include<stdio.h>
/* program to show array use */

int main()

{
    int arr1[8]; /* define an array of 8 integers */
    int i;

    /* ask the user to enter 8 integers */

    printf("enter 8 integer numbers\n");

    for (i = 0;i < 8;i++)
    {
        scanf("%d", &arr1[i]);  /* read the entered integers into
        arr1[i] */
    }
    /* print out the contents of the array */
```

```
        printf("Your 8 numbers are \n");

        for (i = 0;i < 8;i++)
        {
                printf("%d ", arr1[i]);
        }
        printf("\n");

}
```

Create this program and test it. It will read the eight characters you enter and store them in the array "arr1". It then reads arr1 and prints out its contents.

To read and write characters into our array, we define it as "char" and notice that we use %c in our scanf and printf because %c expects characters and %d expects integers.

```
#define _CRT_SECURE_NO_WARNINGS
#include<stdio.h>
/* program to show character array use */

int main()

{
        char arr2[10]; /* define array of 10 characters */
        int i;

        /* ask the user to enter 10 characters */

        printf("enter 10 characters \n");

        for (i = 0;i < 10;i++)
        {
                scanf("%c", &arr2[i]); /* read each character entered into the
                array */
        }
        printf("Your 10 characters are \n");

        /* print out the contents of the array */
```

```
    for (i = 0;i < 10;i++)
    {
        printf("%c ", arr2[i]);
    }
    printf("\n");

}
```

Arrays are really useful when we are writing software to solve mathematics problems. We can extend our ideas we have just learned. If we say that our int array we have just used is in one dimension (i.e., numbers in a line), we can have a two-dimensional array (like numbers in a matrix.)

The following is a program that allows you to enter data into an two-dimensional array. It can have a maximum of eight integers in one part and seven in the other part. This is defined here as int arr1[7][8]. You can picture it like this:

1	2	3	4	5	6	7	8
4	3	4	5	6	7	8	9
0	4	5	6	7	8	9	10
9	5	6	7	8	9	10	11
3	7	8	9	10	11	12	13
8	8	9	10	11	12	13	14
6	9	10	11	12	13	14	15

This array has seven rows and eight columns and can be referred to as a 7x8 array (like a 7x8 matrix in mathematics). Listing 2-8 reads data into the array.

Listing 2-8. c1.2arr2D.c

```
#define _CRT_SECURE_NO_WARNINGS
#include<stdio.h>

/* example of a 2D array test*/
int main()

{
    int arr1[7][8]; /* 2D array */

    int i, j, k, l;

    /* ask the user to enter number of rows and columns to be used */
```

```
printf("enter number of rows and columns (max 7 rows max 8 columns) \n");
scanf("%d %d", &k, &l); /* store the number of rows and columns */

/* test if the user has exceeded the limits for rows or columns */

if (k > 7 || l > 8)
{
    printf("error - max of 8 for rows or columns\n");

}

else
{
    /* ask the user to enter the data for the arrays */

    printf("enter array\n");
    for (i = 0;i < k;i++)
    {
        for (j = 0;j < l;j++)
        {
            scanf("%d", &arr1[i][j]);
        }
    }

    /* print out the 2D array */

    printf("Your array is \n");
    for (i = 0;i < k;i++)
    {
        for (j = 0;j < l;j++)
        {
            printf("%d ", arr1[i][j]);
        }
        printf("\n");

    }
}

}
```

There are a few new ideas in this program. As well as having our two-dimensional array, we also have examples of a nested for loop as seen earlier. We also see something which is a really useful thing to use in your programs. This is called "data vetting." If you look at the definition of our array, its first part has seven integers and its second has eight integers. If the user tried to enter more than eight, it would cause the program to fail with an error. We can prevent this by checking that the user does not enter more than the maximum expected number of integers for each part. This is what the first "if" statement does. The first part of the program stores the number of "rows" into k and the number of columns into l. The if statement says that if the number of rows is greater than seven or the number of columns is greater than eight, then it outputs an error message and terminates the program. The symbol "||" means "or."

The 2D array stores row by row. So if you enter the data shown in the 7x8 matrix shown above and print out the first row, then you should get 1 2 3 4 5 6 7 8. You can write a quick test program to do this.

```c
#define _CRT_SECURE_NO_WARNINGS
#include<stdio.h>

/* example of a 2D array test with extras*/
int main()

{

    int arr1[7][8]; /* 2D array */

    int i, j, k, l;

    /* ask the user to enter number of rows and columns to be used */

    printf("enter number of rows and columns (max 7 rows max 8 columns) \n");
    scanf("%d %d", &k, &l);
    if (k > 7 || l > 8)
    {
        printf("error - max of 8 for rows or columns\n");

    }
```

```
        else
        {
                printf("enter array\n");
                for (i = 0;i < k;i++)
                {
                        for (j = 0;j < l;j++)
                        {
                                scanf("%d", &arr1[i][j]);
                        }
                }
                printf("Your array is \n");
                for (i = 0;i < k;i++)
                {
                        for (j = 0;j < l;j++)
                        {
                                printf("%d ", arr1[i][j]);
                        }
                        printf("\n");

                }
        }

        /* print out the first row of the 2D array */

        printf("first row of array\n");
        for (j = 0;j < l;j++)
        {
                printf("%d ", arr1[0][j]);
        }
        printf("\n");

}
```

This is the same as your 2D array program, except that at the end, it does an extra bit.

```
for(j=0;j<k;j++)
{
        printf("%d ",arr1[0][j]);
}
```

This just prints out arr[0][0], arr[0][1], arr[0][2], arr[0][3], arr[0][4], arr[0][5], arr[0][6], and arr[0][7]. This is how the data is stored in a 2D array. If you wanted the second row, you just need to change the printf("%d",arr1[0][j]); in the last for loop to printf("%d",arr1[1][j]);.

Two-dimensional arrays are vital when you write programs to perform operations on matrices.

$$\begin{pmatrix} 1 & 2 \\ 3 & 4 \\ 5 & 6 \end{pmatrix} + \begin{pmatrix} 2 & 3 \\ 4 & 5 \\ 6 & 7 \end{pmatrix} = \begin{pmatrix} 3 & 5 \\ 7 & 9 \\ 11 & 13 \end{pmatrix}$$

Here we are adding two 3x2 matrices to produce another 3x2 matrix. As you can see from the preceding diagram, we just add the corresponding row and column to produce a sum in the equivalent position in the third matrix.

Listing 2-9 demonstrates this. The first matrix is matarr1 and the second is matarr2. You can see that these are predefined to have the same values as the preceding matrices. The sum of the two is placed into matadd. A nested for loop first clears matadd to zeroes. Another nested for loop performs the addition.

Listing 2-9. c1.2matadd.c

```c
/* Matrix program */
/* add two matrices */
#define _CRT_SECURE_NO_WARNINGS
#include<stdio.h>
int main()
{
    int matarr1[3][2] = {
    {1, 2},
    {3, 4},
    {5, 6}
    };

    int matarr2[3][2] = {
    {2, 3},
    {4, 5},
```

```
{6, 7}
};

 int matadd[3][2];/* matrix answer (rowxcolumn)*/
 int i,j,k;
 int r1,c1,r2,c2;/* row and col for 1st and 2nd matrices */

 r1=3;
 c1=2;
 r2=3;
 c2=2;

 for(i=0;i<r1;i++)
 {
      for(j=0;j<c2;j++)
      {
           matadd[i][j]=0;/* clear the matrix */
      }
 }

 printf("Your first matrix is \n");
 for(i=0;i<r1;i++)
 {
      for(j=0;j<c1;j++)
      {
           printf("%d ",matarr1[i][j]);  /* first matrix in
           matarr1 */
      }
      printf("\n");
 }

 printf("Your second matrix is \n");
 for(i=0;i<r2;i++)
 {
      for(j=0;j<c2;j++)
      {
           printf("%d ",matarr2[i][j]);  /* second matrix in
           matarr2 */
```

```
        }
        printf("\n");
    }
    /* add corresponding elements of the matrices into matadd */
    for(i=0;i<r1;i++)
    {
        for(j=0;j<c2;j++)
        {
            for(k=0;k<r2;k++)
            {
                matadd[i][j] = matarr1[i][j]
                + matarr2[i][j];
            }
        }
    }
    /* Write the solution */
    printf("Your matrix multiplication is \n");
    for(i=0;i<r1;i++)
    {
        for(j=0;j<c2;j++)
        {
            printf("%d ",matadd[i][j]);
        }
        printf("\n");
    }

}
```

The following diagram shows the mechanism for multiplying two matrices. For two matrices, the number of columns of the first matrix must equal the number of rows of the second. For the following matrices, the first matrix is 3x2 (three rows and two columns), and the second matrix is 2x1 (two rows and one column), so these can be multiplied. Looking at the third matrix in the diagram, you can see how the multiplication works.

$$
\begin{pmatrix} 10 & 27 \\ 27 & 31 \\ 48 & 26 \end{pmatrix} \times \begin{pmatrix} 200 \\ 25 \end{pmatrix} = \begin{pmatrix} 10 \times 200 + 27 \times 25 \\ 27 \times 200 + 31 \times 25 \\ 48 \times 200 + 26 \times 25 \end{pmatrix} = \begin{pmatrix} 2675 \\ 6175 \\ 10250 \end{pmatrix}
$$

Listing 2-10 performs the preceding multiplication with two preset matrices, matarr1 and matarr2. The result of the multiplication is held in the matrix matmult. This is cleared to zeroes initially.

Listing 2-10. c1.2matmult4.c

```
/* Matrix program */
/* multiply two matrices */
#define _CRT_SECURE_NO_WARNINGS
#include<stdio.h>
int main()
{
        int matarr1[3][2] = {
        {10, 27},
        {27, 31},
        {48, 26}
        };

        int matarr2[2][1] = {
        {200},
        {25}
        };

        int matmult[3][1]; /* matrix answer (rowxcolumn)*/
        int i,j,k;
        int r1,c1,r2,c2; /* row and col for 1st and 2nd matrices */

        r1=3;
        c1=2;
        r2=2;
        c2=1;
```

```
for(i=0;i<r1;i++)
{
      for(j=0;j<c2;j++)
      {
            matmult[i][j]=0; /* clear the matrix */
      }
}

printf("Your first matrix is \n");
for(i=0;i<r1;i++)
{
      for(j=0;j<c1;j++)
      {
            printf("%d ",matarr1[i][j]); /* first matrix in
            matarr1 */
      }
      printf("\n");
}

printf("Your second matrix is \n");
for(i=0;i<r2;i++)
{
      for(j=0;j<c2;j++)
      {
            printf("%d ",matarr2[i][j]); /* second matrix in
            matarr2 */
      }
      printf("\n");
}
/* multiply corresponding elements of the matrices into matmult */
for(i=0;i<r1;i++)
{
      for(j=0;j<c2;j++)
      {
            for(k=0;k<r2;k++)
            {
```

```
                        matmult[i][j] = matmult[i][j] + matarr1[i][k]
                        * matarr2[k][j];
                }
            }
        }
        /* Write the solution */
        printf("Your matrix multiplication is \n");
        for(i=0;i<r1;i++)
        {
            for(j=0;j<c2;j++)
            {
                printf("%d ",matmult[i][j]);
            }
            printf("\n");
        }

}
```

You have seen the importance of being able to extend our data definitions to include arrays.

Functions

Sometimes when you are writing your programs, you will find that you may end up writing similar lines of code in different places in the program. You can make this easier to do and easier for other people to follow what your code does if you put these similar lines of code in a separate place and just call them when you need them. This separate set of code is called a function. If the function has to do slightly different things each time it gets called, this is fine as you can call the function with a different parameter each time you call it. The following code will demonstrate this. It is a fairly trivial piece of code, but it illustrates the point.

```
#define _CRT_SECURE_NO_WARNINGS
#include <stdio.h>

/* This code demonstrates what a function does */
/* The function here compares two numbers and says which is bigger */
/* The user enters three numbers and gets told which is bigger than
which !*/
```

```
        void myfunction(int a,int b); /* declaration of your function and its
        parameters */

        int first , second, third;
main()
{
        /* ask the user to enter the three numbers to be compared */

        printf( "Please enter first integer number: " );
        scanf( "%d", &first );
        printf( "Please enter second integer number: " );
        scanf( "%d", &second );
        printf( "Please enter third integer number: " );
        scanf( "%d", &third );

        myfunction(first , second); /* compare the first with the second */
        myfunction(first , third); /* compare the first with the third */
        myfunction(second , third); /* compare the second with the third */
}
void myfunction(int a,int b)
/* the function is outside the main{} part of the program */
/* The function just compares the two parameters, a and b, and says which
is greater*/
{

        if(a>b)
                printf("%d is greater than %d\n", a,b);
        else if (a<b)
                printf("%d is greater than %d\n", b,a);
        else
                printf("%d and %d are equal\n", a,b);
}
```

The function here is called myfunction. Notice that it is defined outside of main{}.
It is declared at the start of the program. The function is given two numbers, a and b. It
compares the two numbers and says which is bigger. In the main part of the program,
the user is prompted to enter three numbers. These are then entered into the calls to
myfunction in the main part of the code.

This is a fairly simple piece of code, but it shows how a function can be used.

Listing 2-11 also shows how functions are used. This code is based on the program you wrote in the "Data Arrays" section of this chapter. It prints out specific rows of your 2D array. One call to the function asks the function to print out the second row of the array, and the other call asks it to print out the first row.

Listing 2-11. c1.2func.c

```
#define _CRT_SECURE_NO_WARNINGS
#include<stdio.h>

/* example of a function*/
void printarow(int row, int cols, int arr[8][8]);
int main()

{
    int arr1[8][8];

    int i, j, rows, cols;

    /* ask the user to enter the rows and columns */

    printf("enter number of rows and columns (max 8 rows max 8 columns)
    \n");
    scanf("%d %d", &rows, &cols);
    if (rows > 8 || cols > 8)
    {
        printf("error - max of 8 for rows or columns\n");

    }

    else
    {
        printf("enter array\n");
        for (i = 0;i < rows;i++)
        {
            for (j = 0;j < cols;j++)
            {
                scanf("%d", &arr1[i][j]);
```

```
                    }
             }
             printf("Your array is \n");
             for (i = 0;i < rows;i++)
             {
                    for (j = 0;j < cols;j++)
                    {
                           printf("%d ", arr1[i][j]);
                    }
                    printf("\n");

             }
      }
      printarow(2, cols, arr1); /* This calls to print out row 2
      only(assumes that you have at least 2 rows) */
      printf("\n");
      printarow(1, cols, arr1); /* This calls to print out row 1 only */
      printf("\n");
}

void      printarow(int row, int cols, int arr[8][8])

/* this is a function which can be called from anywhere in the program */
/* and can be called as often as you want to */
/* If you need to do the same type of thing many times it saves you */
/* having to write out the same code repeatedly. All you need to */
/* is call the function */

{
      int j;
      printf("row %d is ", row);
      for (j = 0;j < cols;j++)
      {
             printf("%d ", arr[row - 1][j]);
      }

}
```

Notice that the array name used in the function does not have to be the same as that used in main{}. In the instruction if(rows>7 || cols>8), the || means OR. So here, we are saying if the user has specified more than seven rows or more than eight columns, then we print an error and stop the program. At the end of the chapter, the common arithmetic and logical symbols used in C are listed.

Create and test this program. The code assumes you have at least two rows. You could amend the code to call printarow as many times as you want to.

A function can return a value to the caller. The following code demonstrates this:

```c
/* Function which returns an answer  */
/* finds the pupil in one year of the school with the highest marks */

#include <stdio.h>
double getmarks(double pupils[]);

int main()
{
    double pupil;
    /* Array with marks for class is preset in the main part of the
       program */
    double marks[] = { 10.6, 23.7, 67.9, 93.0, 64.2, 33.8 ,57.5 ,82.2
    ,50.7 ,45.7 };

    /* Call function getmarks. The function returns the max marks which
       is then stored in pupil */
    pupil = getmarks(marks);
    printf("Max mark is  = %f", pupil);
    return 0;
}

double getmarks(double pupils[])
{
    int i;
    double highest;
    highest = 0;
    /* Go through all the pupils in turn and store the highest mark */
    for (i = 0; i < 6; ++i)
```

```
    {
        if (highest < pupils[i])
            highest = pupils[i];

    }
    return highest; /* returns the value in highest to where the function
    was called */
}
```

The function is called getmarks. It returns a value to the point where it was called. In real-life programs, the function will be called many times from different points in the program. This technique is both efficient and makes the program easier to follow.

Strings

Strings in C are just like character arrays we have already looked at. The main difference is that the string has a NULL character at the end. This is just to show where the string ends as we have to do things like compare two strings or find the length of the string. To find the length, we have a function written for us in the string.h library, and this needs to NULL character at the end. As a result of this, if we are defining a preset string as a character array of a certain length, we need to account for the NULL at the end. So if our string had "tokens" in it, the word has six characters so our string array would have to have seven characters in its definition to account for the NULL character at the end. When we print a string using printf, we use %s to show it is a string (where we used %d to print an integer or %f to print a floating point number).

Listing 2-12 is a program to check the length of strings (strlen), copy on to another (strcpy), concatenate two strings (strcat), and compare the contents of two strings (strcmp).

Concatenation of two strings is just tagging one string onto the end of the other.

Listing 2-12. c1.2string.c

```
#define _CRT_SECURE_NO_WARNINGS
#include <stdio.h>
#include <string.h>
/* Program to demonstrate string operations strlen, strcpy, strcat,
strcmp */
```

```
int main() {
    char borrow[7] = { 't', 'o', 'k', 'e', 'n', 's','\0' };
    char string1[32] = "This is string1";
    char string2[16] = "This is string2";
    char string3[16];
    int  len;
    /* Print out the lengths of the strings */

    len = strlen(string1);
    printf("strlen(string1) :  %d\n", len);
    len = strlen(string2);
    printf("strlen(string2) :  %d\n", len);
    len = strlen(string3);
    printf("strlen(string3) :  %d\n", len);

    /* copy string1 into string3 */

    strcpy(string3, string1);
    printf("strcpy( string3, string1) :  %s\n", string3);
    len = strlen(string3);
    printf("strlen(string3) after copy of string1 into string3 :  %d\n",
    len);

    /* Compare string1 and string3 (these should be the same)*/

    if (strcmp(string1, string3) == 0)
        printf("strings are the same\n");

    /* concatenates string1 and string2 */

    strcat(string1, string2);
    printf("strcat( string1, string2):   %s\n", string1);

    /* total length of string1 after concatenation */

    len = strlen(string1);
    printf("strlen(string1) after cat of string2 onto string1 :  %d\n",
    len);
```

```
    printf("String as predefined quoted chars: %s\n", borrow);

    return 0;
}
```

In strlen, the function returns the length of the string.

In strcpy, the function copies the second string in the command to the first.

In strcmp, the function compares the contents of the two strings and returns 0 if they are equal.

In strcat, the function tags the second string onto the end of the first string.

This section has demonstrated string use in C. An extension of this is the definition of "structures" which is shown in the following.

Structures

The variables used up to now have just been singly named variables of a certain type. Another type of variable is a structure. This is a variable that contains separate variables within it. If you imagine a file containing details of a student at a college, the details of each student might be their name, their student ID, and possibly their last examination mark. So, in a paper file, these may be held like this:

```
id
Name
Percent
```

So there would be an entry like this in the file for each student.

Here is a program which declares such a structure. It then assigns variable names s1 and s2 to have that type of definition. Then it gives each structure values and then prints them out.

```
/* Structure example program */
#define _CRT_SECURE_NO_WARNINGS
#include<stdio.h>
#include<string.h>

/* define the structure */
struct Student {
    int id;
```

```
        char name[16];
        double percent;
};

int main() {
        /* define two data locations of type "student" */

        struct Student s1, s2;

        /* Assign values to the s1 structure */

        s1.id = 56;
        strcpy(s1.name, "Rob Smith");
        s1.percent = 67.400000;
        /* Print out structure s1 */

        printf("\nid : %d", s1.id);
        printf("\nName : %s", s1.name);
        printf("\nPercent : %lf", s1.percent);

        /* Assign values to the s2 structure */

        s2.id = 73;
        strcpy(s2.name, "Mary Gallagher");
        s2.percent = 93.800000;

        /* Print out structure s1 */

        printf("\nid : %d", s2.id);
        printf("\nName : %s", s2.name);
        printf("\nPercent : %lf", s2.percent);

        return (0);
}
```

This can be extended, so instead of defining individual entries (s1 and s2), we can define a larger number in one definition. In the following example, we define five items in the array year9. Then we refer to the first student entry as year9[0], the second student entry as year9[1], etc. (Listing 2-13).

Listing 2-13. c1.2struct.c

```c
/* Structure example program (extended structure)*/
#define _CRT_SECURE_NO_WARNINGS
#include<stdio.h>

/* define the structure */

struct Student {
    int id;
    char name[16];
    double percent;
};
int main() {
      int i;
    /* define 5 data locations of type "student" */
        struct Student year9[5];
        for(i=0; i<5; i++)
        {
            /* Assign values to the structure */
            printf("enter student ID\n");
            scanf("%d",&year9[i].id);
            printf("enter student name\n");
            scanf("%s",year9[i].name);
            printf("enter student percent\n");
            scanf("%lf",&year9[i].percent);
        }
        for(i=0; i<5; i++)
        {
            /* Print out structure s1 */

            printf("\nid : %d", year9[i].id);
            printf("\nName : %s", year9[i].name);
            printf("\nPercent : %lf", year9[i].percent);

        }
    return (0);
}
```

This type of structure definition is vital when you set up files and write them or read them. You will see more of structures in the chapter dealing with file usage.

Structures are used widely in file handling.

Size of Variables

There is a useful function in C which tells you the size in bytes of variables on your machine. Sometimes, different compilers or software development tools have different sizes for different structures. The function is called sizeof. You supply it with the variable type you want to know the size of, and it returns the answer as the number of bytes.

You can also supply a structure as the parameter if you don't know its size (Listing 2-14).

Listing 2-14. sizeof

```
/* Program to illustrate the use of the sizeof command */

#include <stdio.h >
#include < limits.h >
#include < math.h >

    int main() {

    int sizeofint;
    unsigned int sizeofunsint;
    float sizeoffloat;
    double sizeofdouble;
    char sizeofchar;

    printf("storage size for int : %zd \n", sizeof(sizeofint));
    printf("storage size for uns int : %zd \n", sizeof(sizeofunsint));
    printf("storage size for float : %zd \n", sizeof(sizeoffloat));
    printf("storage size for double float: %zd \n",
    sizeof(sizeofdouble));
    printf("storage size for char: %zd \n", sizeof(sizeofchar));

    return(0);

}
```

This prints out the sizes of an int, an unsigned int, a floating point, and a double floating point as follows:

```
storage size for int : 4
storage size for uns int : 4
storage size for float : 4
storage size for double float: 8
storage size for char: 1
```

Goto Command

Under some circumstances, you may want to jump out of your normal sequence of code, for instance, if you discover an error in a sequence of code. In this case, you can define a label and jump to the label from within your sequence of code.

Goto is not used frequently in programming but can be used if you want a quick exit from your program (Listing 2-15).

Listing 2-15. c1.2goto.c

```
/* Demonstrate a goto statement */
/* a:, b:, c:,d:,e:, f:is a simulation of a program. We will simulate an
   error by setting testvalue to 2*/

#define _CRT_SECURE_NO_WARNINGS
#include <stdio.h>
int main()
{
    int i, testvalue;
    int x1,x2,x3,x4,x5,x6;

    printf("Please enter a number:\n ");
    scanf("%d", &testvalue); /* read number in */

    x1 = x2 = x3 = x4 = x5 = x6 = 0;

    a:
        x1 = 1;

    b:
        x2 = 1;
        if(testvalue == 2)
```

```
            goto f;
    c:
        x3 = 1;
    d:
        x4 = 1;
    e:
        x5 = 1;
    f:
        x6 = 1;

    printf("x1 = %d, x2 = %d, x3 = %d, x4 = %d, x5 = %d, x6 = %d,
        \n",x1,x2,x3,x4,x5,x6);
}
```

This outputs (if you enter 0, 3456, and 2)

```
Please enter a number:
 0
x1 = 1, x2 = 1, x3 = 1, x4 = 1, x5 = 1, x6 = 1,
Please enter a number:
 3456
x1 = 1, x2 = 1, x3 = 1, x4 = 1, x5 = 1, x6 = 1,
Please enter a number:
 2
x1 = 1, x2 = 1, x3 = 0, x4 = 0, x5 = 0, x6 = 1,
```

Common Mathematical and Logical Symbols

The following is a list of mathematical symbols used in C code and their meanings:

```
=   assign
==  equals
!=  not equal to
<   less than
>   greater than
<= less than or equal to
>=  greater than or equal to
```

```
&&   logical AND
||   logical OR
!    logical NOT
```

File Access

This section is about moving data to and from files. The basic commands of file access are fopen (which opens a file), fclose (which closes it), fread (which reads data from a file which has been opened), and fwrite (which writes data to a file which has been opened). There are one or two other file commands which we shall meet later.

We will have a look at these techniques here.

We declare the pointer at the start of the program using the instruction FILE *fp. The asterisk, *, signifies that the variable is a pointer, and whenever we access the file in our program, we use fp. We set up the value of the pointer using the fopen command.

"w" means we want write access to the file. The possible values in fopen for this are as follows:

"r" = opens for reading

"w" = creates a file for writing

"a" = append to a file

"r+" = read and write

"w+" = creates a file for reading and writing

"a+" = opens for reading and appending

The fopen command returns a pointer, and this is stored in fp. The code is shown in the following.

In this program, we are using the command fwrite to write to the file.

```
fwrite(&s10, sizeof(s1), 1, fp);
```

We write the data in s10 to the file pointed to by fp. When we have written all of our data to the file, we call

```
fclose(fp);
```

This closes the file pointed to by fp.

Student Records File

Our next program in this chapter shows how we can write a structure containing different types of data to a file. The data contains student identifier, their name, and their examination marks. The structure is shown as follows:

```
struct student {
        int studentID;
        char name[13];
        int marks;
};
```

There is one of these structures for each student. The first program creates a file containing this data. The structure data for each student is set at the beginning of the program.

We start by opening the file. The instruction is

```
fp = fopen("students.bin", "w");
```

where students.bin is the filename and fp is the file pointer.

We write to the file using several fwrite calls.

We close the file and then reopen it in order to check what we have written. In our read, we have

```
numread=fread(&s2, sizeof(s2), 1, fp);
```

where numread is the number of structures read. We are expecting one structure to have been read as shown by the third parameter in our fread. If it is 1, then we print the record. If it is not 1, we check the error. By calling the command feof(fp), we can check if we have had an unexpected end of file. If so, then we print out an appropriate message.

Finally, we close the file (Listing 2-16).

Listing 2-16. c1.2filewrite2.c

```
/* Create the file and write records to it */

#define _CRT_SECURE_NO_WARNINGS
#include<stdio.h>

/*define the structure for each student's data */
```

```
struct student {
     int studentID;
     char name[13];
     int marks;
};

int main()
{
     int i, numread;
     FILE *fp;
     struct student s1;
     struct student s2;

     /* Preset the data for each student */

     struct student s10 = { 10,"Coster      ",15 };
     struct student s11 = { 11,"Harris      ",20 };
     struct student s12 = { 12,"Frazer      ",25 };
     struct student s13 = { 13,"Kirrane     ",30 };
     struct student s14 = { 14,"Marley      ",35 };
     struct student s15 = { 15,"OBrien      ",40 };
     struct student s16 = { 16,"Brown       ",45 };
     struct student s17 = { 17,"Tomlinson   ",50 };
     struct student s18 = { 18,"Mulcahy     ",55 };
     struct student s19 = { 19,"Coyle       ",60 };
     struct student s20 = { 20,"Baxter      ",65 };
     struct student s21 = { 21,"Weeks       ",70 };
     struct student s22 = { 22,"Owens       ",75 };
     struct student s23 = { 23,"Cannon      ",80 };
     struct student s24 = { 24,"Parker      ",85 };

     /* Open the students file */

     fp = fopen("students.bin", "w");

     /* Write details of each student to file*/
     /* from the structures defined above */
```

```
fwrite(&s10, sizeof(s1), 1, fp);
fwrite(&s11, sizeof(s1), 1, fp);
fwrite(&s12, sizeof(s1), 1, fp);
fwrite(&s13, sizeof(s1), 1, fp);
fwrite(&s14, sizeof(s1), 1, fp);
fwrite(&s15, sizeof(s1), 1, fp);
fwrite(&s16, sizeof(s1), 1, fp);
fwrite(&s17, sizeof(s1), 1, fp);
fwrite(&s18, sizeof(s1), 1, fp);
fwrite(&s19, sizeof(s1), 1, fp);
fwrite(&s20, sizeof(s1), 1, fp);
fwrite(&s21, sizeof(s1), 1, fp);
fwrite(&s22, sizeof(s1), 1, fp);
fwrite(&s23, sizeof(s1), 1, fp);
fwrite(&s24, sizeof(s1), 1, fp);
```

/* Close the file */

```
fclose(fp);
```

/* Reopen the file (at the start of the file)*/

```
fopen("students.bin", "r");
```

/* Read and print out all of the records on the file */

```
for (i = 0;i < 15;i++)
{
     numread = fread(&s2, sizeof(s2), 1, fp);    /* read into
     structure s2 */

     if (numread == 1)
     {
          /* reference elements of structure by s2.studentID etc */

          printf("\nstudentID : %d", s2.studentID);
          printf("\nName : %s", s2.name);
          printf("\nmarks : %d", s2.marks);
     }
```

```
        else {
                /* If an error occurred on read then print out message */

                if (feof(fp))

                        printf("Error reading students.bin : unexpected end
                        of file fp is %p\n", fp);

                else if (ferror(fp))
                {
                        perror("Error reading students.bin");
                }
        }

    }
    /* Close the file */

    fclose(fp);


}
```

Listing 2-17 reads and displays the data from the file. Again, we open the file, this time as read-only ("r" in the open call).

The following code shows this.

We specify in the fread that we want to read the data into the structure in our program. Here the structure is s2, and at the top of the program, we have our structure definition as for the filewrite program. In our definition of s2, we identify it as type "structure student." This defines the type in the same way as int defines the type for our numread as in definitions at the top of the program.

Listing 2-17. c1.2fileread3.c

```
/* fileread */
/* reads from file */
/* reads and prints sequentially */

#define _CRT_SECURE_NO_WARNINGS
#include<stdio.h>

/*define the structure for each student's data */
```

```c
struct student {
      int studentID;
      char name[13];
      int marks;
};

int main()
{
      FILE *fp;

      struct student s2;

      int numread, i;
      /* Open students file */

      fp = fopen("students.bin", "r");
      printf("\nAll students\n");
      for (i = 0;i < 15;i++)
      {
            /* Read each student data from file sequentially */

            fread(&s2, sizeof(s2), 1, fp);

            /* Print student ID, name and Marks for each student */

            printf("\nstudentID : %d", s2.studentID);
            printf("\n Name : %s", s2.name);
            printf("\nmarks : %d", s2.marks);

      }

      fclose(fp);

}
```

Listing 2-18 shows how to update a record in the file. Here we want to update the student's record whose ID is 23 and add 10 to their marks. We move through the file until we find the correct ID. We then add 10 to their marks in their structure. At this point, the file pointer is pointing to the next record, so we have to move it back one record, and then our fwrite will overwrite the correct record. We move back by one record using the command

```
fseek(fp,minusone*sizeof(s2),SEEK_CUR);
```

The minusone*sizeof(s2) part of this instruction means go backward by the length of one record.

Listing 2-18. c1.2fileupdate2.c

```
/* fileupdate */
/* reads and prints sequentially */
/* reads, updates and prints specific records */

#define _CRT_SECURE_NO_WARNINGS
#include<stdio.h>
/*define the structure for each student's data */

struct student {
      int studentID;
      char name[13];
      int marks;
};

int main()
{
      FILE *fp;
      long int minusone = -1;
      struct student s2;

      int numread, i;
      /* Open students file */

      fp = fopen("students.bin", "r");
      printf("\nAll students\n");
      for (i = 0;i < 15;i++)
      {
            /* Read each student data from file sequentially */

            fread(&s2, sizeof(s2), 1, fp);
```

/* **Print student ID, name and marks for each student** */

```
        printf("\nstudentID : %d", s2.studentID);
        printf("\n Name : %s", s2.name);
        printf("\nmarks : %d", s2.marks);

    }

    fclose(fp);
```

/* **Re-open the students file** */

```
    fp = fopen("students.bin", "r+");   /* r+ is for update */
    printf("\nStudent ID=23\n");

    for (i = 0;i < 15;i++)
    {
        /* Search the file for student with ID of 23 */

        fread(&s2, sizeof(s2), 1, fp);
        if (s2.studentID == 23)
        {
            /* Found the student. */
            /* update their marks */
            /* Print their updated details */

            s2.marks = s2.marks + 10;
            printf("\nName : %s", s2.name);
            printf("\nmarks : %d", s2.marks);
            fseek(fp,minusone*sizeof(s2),SEEK_CUR);
            fwrite(&s2,sizeof(s2),1,fp);
            break;
        }
    }
    /* Go back to the beginning of the file */

    fseek(fp, sizeof(s2), SEEK_END);
    rewind(fp);
    printf("\updated file\n");
```

/* read and display the updated file*/

```
for (i = 0;i < 15;i++)
{
        fread(&s2, sizeof(s2), 1, fp);
        printf("\nName : %s", s2.name);
        printf("\nmarks : %d", s2.marks);

}

fclose(fp);


}
```

Listing 2-19 shows how we can select specific records or numbers of records from the file. We open the file using fp = fopen("students.bin", "r");. The "r" here means read-only.

We start by reading all of the files and printing out all of the data. We then close the file and reopen it. We want to find the student whose ID is 23. When we find it, we print it out.

Rather than closing our file and reopening it, we can call rewind which sets the file back to the beginning. We use fseek(fp, sizeof(s2), SEEK_END); to get to the end of the file and then rewind(fp); to move the file pointer back to the beginning.

On this pass of the file, we want to find all of the students whose marks are above 63. We, again, set up a for loop to look through each structure on the file. If the marks are over 63, we print out the student's name. This time we don't break from the for loop because there may be more than one student with marks over 63.

We then rewind to the start of the program and print out the first three students in the file. This program shows some of the different select options we have.

Listing 2-19. c1.2fileselect.c

```
/* fileupdate */
/* reads from file */
/* reads and prints sequentially */
/* reads and prints specific records */

#define _CRT_SECURE_NO_WARNINGS
#include<stdio.h>
```

/*define the structure for each student's data */

```
struct student {
      int studentID;
      char name[13];
      int marks;
};

int main()
{
      FILE *fp;
      long int minusone = -1;
      struct student s2;

      int numread, i;
```

      /* Open students file */

```
      fp = fopen("students.bin", "r");
      printf("\nAll students\n");
      for (i = 0;i < 15;i++)
      {
```

            /* Read each student data from file sequentially */

```
            fread(&s2, sizeof(s2), 1, fp);
```

            /* Print student ID, name and marks for each student */

```
            printf("\nstudentID : %d", s2.studentID);
            printf("\n Name : %s", s2.name);
            printf("\nmarks : %d", s2.marks);

      }

      fclose(fp);
```

      /* Re-open the students file */

```
      fp = fopen("students.bin", "r");
      printf("\nStudent ID=23\n");
```

```c
for (i = 0;i < 15;i++)
{
        /* Search the file for student with ID of 23 */

        fread(&s2, sizeof(s2), 1, fp);
        if (s2.studentID == 23)
        {
                /* Found the student. Print their name and marks */

                printf("\nName : %s", s2.name);
                printf("\nmarks : %d", s2.marks);

                break;
        }
}
/* Go back to the beginning of the file */

fseek(fp, sizeof(s2), SEEK_END);
rewind(fp);
printf("\nStudents marks>63\n");

/* Find all students with marks are above 63 */

for (i = 0;i < 15;i++)
{
fread(&s2, sizeof(s2), 1, fp);
    if (s2.marks > 63)
    {
            /* Print out name of each student with marks above 63 */
            printf("\nName : %s", s2.name);

    }
}
/* Go back to the beginning of the file */

rewind(fp);

/* Read and print out the first 3 students in the file */
```

```c
        printf("\nFirst 3 students \n");

        numread = fread(&s2, sizeof(s2), 1, fp);
        if (numread == 1)
        {
                printf("\nstudentID : %d", s2.studentID);
                printf("\nName : %s", s2.name);
                printf("\nmarks : %d", s2.marks);
        }
        numread = fread(&s2, sizeof(s2), 1, fp);
        if (numread == 1)
        {
                printf("\nstudentID : %d", s2.studentID);
                printf("\nName : %s", s2.name);
                printf("\nmarks : %d", s2.marks);
        }
        numread = fread(&s2, sizeof(s2), 1, fp);
        if (numread == 1)
        {
                printf("\nstudentID : %d", s2.studentID);
                printf("\nName : %s", s2.name);
                printf("\nmarks : %d", s2.marks);
        }
        /* Close the file */

        fclose(fp);

}
```

Summary

After reading this chapter and running the programs shown, you should have a good understanding of how C can help you in your work. The following chapters implement what has been shown in Chapter 1 and here.

Exercises

1. For your for loop example, in your for loop program, read in an integer number and use it in your for instruction as the limit for the loop. Test your amendment by giving it the same number as your original for loop program.

2. Write a program to extend the data array program so that you enter and store two separate arrays. Then print out the first line of the first array and the first line of the second array.

3. Write a program similar to the one where you return a value from a function. In this case, the function is called to find the average of a set of marks. Set up an array in the main part of the program and initialize it with nine values. Call your function to calculate the average of these numbers. Your function should return the average, and this value is stored in the main part of the program and then printed out.

4. Write a program to add another student to the file. Do not just add it to the list in the c1.2filewrite2.c program, but write a new program to append another student to the file.

CHAPTER 3

SQL in C

This chapter introduces the reader to the way the database language, Structured Query Language (SQL), can be accessed and used from a C program. It will be demonstrated how to create the database file. When this is done, the reader will be able to create database tables. Then, it will be shown how to insert data into the table, how to amend data in the table, how to delete data from the table, and how to print out data held in the table.

Review of SQL and SQLite

SQL (Structured Query Language) is used to access a database. The easiest way to understand this is to look at an example of a database table. One such table is shown in the following. This is the table we will use in this chapter.

A typical database table would contain information about a large number of people working for the same company. The data for one person is contained in a "row." This row holds the person's ID, their surname, their age, and their job title (occupation).

id	surname	age	occupation
123	Jones	37	Accountant
125	Smith	42	HR
128	Allen	28	Secretary
131	Bradley	26	Programmer
132	Edwards	41	Programmer
133	King	35	S/W Engineer
134	Price	39	H/W Engineer
136	Roberts	52	Manager

(continued)

© Philip Joyce 2022
P. Joyce, *C and Python Applications*, https://doi.org/10.1007/978-1-4842-7774-4_3

id	surname	age	occupation
138	Foster	44	Analyst
139	Shannon	24	Programmer
141	Lewis	27	Receptionist

We will use sqlite3 which is a relational database management system. This is in a C library which acts as our interface to SQL. If sqlite3 is not on your computer, it is downloadable free of charge.

Creating the Database

Create the database using the following code in a C program (creating and running a C program are shown in Chapter 2):

```
dbcreate = sqlite3_open("test.db",&db);
```

After this call, dbcreate will contain 0 if the database is opened successfully and non-zero otherwise.

If the database file is created or it already exists, then this command returns its pointer in "db".

This creates the database file test.db in the current directory. We can use the same name for the database file and one of its tables.

We use SQL to create the table. In the preceding case, we will call the table "Personnel", so the SQL command for this would be

```
CREATE TABLE Personnel (id INT PRIMARY KEY, surname TEXT, age INT,
occupation);
```

In this case, the ID is the "Primary Key" which uniquely identifies the person. So, for example, if two people had the same surname, then as their primary keys would be different, this would uniquely identify them.

We create the row for each person by having a separate "INSERT" statement for each of them. The first person in our table could be defined by the following statement

```
INSERT INTO Personnel  VALUES (123, 'Jones', 37, 'Accountant');
```

where 123 is the id, 'Jones' is the surname, 37 is the age, and 'Accountant' is the occupation.

If we wanted to find the names of all of the programmers in the company, then we would use a SELECT SQL statement which would say

```
SELECT surname FROM Personnel WHERE occupation = 'Programmer';
```

We can select a specific group using the "HAVING" option. In the following case, we want to select everybody whose age is greater than 25. Here, the "*" in the command means "everybody."

```
SELECT * FROM Personnel GROUP BY age HAVING age > 25
```

We can amend a row using the "UPDATE" command. In the case shown in the following, we want to update the person's occupation to be 'manager':

```
UPDATE Personnel SET  occupation = 'manager' WHERE id = 123;
```

Finally, we can delete a row by specifying the ID of the row to be deleted in the "DELETE" command shown here:

```
DELETE FROM Personnel WHERE id = 136;
```

We will use the sqlite3 standard software.

The C programs in this chapter use the fundamental SQL interface routines supplied when you download sqlite3.

The three main interface routines used are **sqlite3_open**, **sqlite3_exec**, and **sqlite3_close**:

1) sqlite3_open("test.db", &db); connects to the test.db database file. This returns a value to say if the connection was successful.

2) sqlite3_exec(db, sql, callback, 0, &err_msg); executes the SQL command held in the "sql" parameter. The "callback" parameter can be 0, or it can be the name of a function that is called when the sqlite3_exec function returns. This function can then process the rows that sqlite3_exec has retrieved. &err_msg returns any error message.

3) sqlite3_close(db); closes the database connection.

   When sqlite3_open returns a successful connection to the database file, then we can create a new table in the file or access an existing one.

4) sqlite3_errmsg(db) gives an error message.

```
#include <sqlite3.h>
#include <stdio.h>
```

These are the two include files we need for the programs used here.

In the programs, the char *sql is a command which sets up a pointer to where the program stores the command (CREATE, SELECT, etc.).

After the exec statement is performed, the status of the command is held in rc. This is then checked, and if there is an error, it can be reported to the user using err_msg.

SQLITE_OK is zero.

Programs return 1 if there has been an error or 0 otherwise.

Having seen these basic ideas, we can now proceed to write the programs.

Creating a Table

This program creates the "Personnel" table as described earlier.

The actual database is the file "test.db". Our database tables are added into this.

In Listing 3-1, the data for each of the eight rows to be inserted is coded into the program. In later programs, we will allow the user to enter the data manually from the command line.

Listing 3-1. csqlinsert_datax.c

```
#include <sqlite3.h>
#include <stdio.h>
int main(void)
{
sqlite3 *db;
char *err_msg = 0;
```

```
int rc = sqlite3_open("test.db", &db);/* open the database */

/* check the status of the database open request */

if (rc != SQLITE_OK)
    {
    /* database cannot be opened */
    /* report the error */
    fprintf(stderr, "Cannot open database: %s\n",
    sqlite3_errmsg(db));
    sqlite3_close(db);
    return 1;
}

/* The database exists so we can create our table and add our 8 rows to
    it */
/* The 'create table' and 8 'insert' commands can be */
/* copied into the *sql pointer together */
/* Each row contains ID, Name, Age and Occupation */

char *sql = "DROP TABLE IF EXISTS Personnel;"
"CREATE TABLE Personnel(Id INT PRIMARY KEY, Name TEXT,       Age INT,
Occupation);"
"INSERT INTO Personnel VALUES(1, 'Brown', 42,      'accountant');"
"INSERT INTO Personnel VALUES(2, 'Jones', 27,      'programmer');"
"INSERT INTO Personnel VALUES(3, 'White', 30,      'engineer');"
"INSERT INTO Personnel VALUES(4, 'Green', 29,      'electrician');"
"INSERT INTO Personnel VALUES(5, 'Smith', 35,      'manager');"
"INSERT INTO Personnel VALUES(6, 'Black', 21,      'secretary');"
"INSERT INTO Personnel VALUES(7, 'Allen', 41,      'cleaner');"
"INSERT INTO Personnel VALUES(8, 'Stone', 21,      'receptionist');";

rc = sqlite3_exec(db, sql, 0, 0, &err_msg); /* perform the create table
and inserts and check if any errors */

if (rc != SQLITE_OK )
{
    /* an error has occurred - report it and close program */
```

```
        fprintf(stderr, "SQL error: %s\n", err_msg);
        sqlite3_free(err_msg);
        sqlite3_close(db);
        return 1;
    }
    sqlite3_close(db); /* close the database connection */
    return 0;
}
```

You can print the whole table by using the program **Csqlselect_allx2b.c** described in the section "Selecting All Rows" in this chapter.

If we print out the table, it would look like this:

```
Id = 1
Name = Brown
Age = 42
Occupation = accountant

Id = 2
Name = Jones
Age = 27
Occupation = programmer

Id = 3
Name = White
Age = 30
Occupation = engineer

Id = 4
Name = Green
Age = 29
Occupation = electrician

Id = 5
Name = Smith
Age = 35
Occupation = manager
```

```
Id = 6
Name = Black
Age = 21
Occupation = secretary

Id = 7
Name = Allen
Age = 41
Occupation = cleaner

Id = 8
Name = Stone
Age = 21
Occupation = receptionist
```

We will see how to write code to print out the contents of the table in the section "Selecting All Rows."

Having created the table, we will now see how to insert, amend, and delete data.

Inserting Rows

Now that we have our database table with its rows, we may want to add another row (if, say, the company has just recruited a new employee).

Insert a Preset Row

Listing 3-2 inserts a preset row. Again, the data for the new row is coded into the program.

Listing 3-2. csqlinsert_onex.c

```c
#include <sqlite3.h>
#include <stdio.h>
int main(void)
{
sqlite3 *db;
char *err_msg = 0;
int rc = sqlite3_open("test.db", &db); );/* open the database */
```

```
/* check the status of the database open request */

if (rc != SQLITE_OK)
{
    fprintf(stderr, "Cannot open database: %s\n",
    sqlite3_errmsg(db));
    sqlite3_close(db);
    return 1;
}

/* Insert our new row with ID=9 name=Wells, age=49 and occupation = teacher
   */

char *sql = "INSERT INTO Personnel VALUES(9, 'Wells', 49, 'teacher');"; /*
set up the insert instruction */

rc = sqlite3_exec(db, sql, 0, 0, &err_msg); /* perform the insert */
if (rc != SQLITE_OK )
{
    /* an error has occurred - report it and close program */
    fprintf(stderr, "SQL error: %s\n", err_msg);
    sqlite3_free(err_msg);
    sqlite3_close(db);
    return 1;
}
sqlite3_close(db); /* close the database connection */
return 0;
}
```

Inserting a User-Entered Row

This next program, shown in Listing 3-3, inserts one user-entered row. The user is prompted to enter the ID, name, age, and occupation. Assume that the user enters "12" for ID, "Pickford" for name, "48" for age, and "Welder" for occupation. The INSERT INTO Personnel VALUES(12, 'Pickford', 48, 'Welder'); statement is concatenated together in the program using the four user-entered data items. The commas, brackets, and quotes in the preceding INSERT statement are added individually.

Listing 3-3. csqlinsert_onex2.c

```c
#include <sqlite3.h>
#include <stdio.h>
int main(void)
{
sqlite3 *db;
char *err_msg = 0;

int idin,agein; /store areas for ID and age */
char namein[13]; /store area for name */
char occupin[15]; /store area for occupation */

int rc = sqlite3_open("test.db", &db);/* open the database */
if (rc != SQLITE_OK)
{
    fprintf(stderr, "Cannot open database: %s\n",
    sqlite3_errmsg(db));
    sqlite3_close(db);
    return 1;
}

/* user is asked to enter the fields for this row */
printf("enter  id \n"); /* ID */
scanf("%d", &idin);
printf("enter name id \n"); /* NAME */
scanf("%s", &namein);
printf("enter age \n"); /* AGE */
scanf("%d", &agein);
printf("enter occupation \n"); /* OCCUPATION */
scanf("%s", &occupin);

/* The INSERT command string is set up */
char str1[200] = "INSERT INTO Personnel VALUES( ";
char str2[] = " ); ";
char str3[2];
char str4[6];
```

```
char str5[] = ", ";
char str6[] = "'";

sprintf(str4, "%d", idin); /* ID value as a string */
sprintf(str3, "%d", agein); /* age value as a string */

/* str1 will be the string containing the complete INSERT command */

strcat(str1,str4); /* ID */
strcat(str1,str5); /* comma */
strcat(str1,str6); /* quote */
strcat(str1,namein); /* name */
strcat(str1,str6); /* quote */
strcat(str1,str5); /* comma */
strcat(str1,str3); /* age */
strcat(str1,str5); /* comma */
strcat(str1,str6); /* quote */
strcat(str1,occupin); /* occupation */
strcat(str1,str6); /* quote */
strcat(str1,str2); /* close bracket and semi-colon */

printf(str1); /* completed string */

/* so, for ID=12, name=Pickford, age=48 and occupation = Welder */
/* our completed string will be :- */
/* INSERT INTO Personnel VALUES( 12, 'Pickford', 48, 'Welder' ); */

char *sql = str1; /* move the completed string to *sql */

rc = sqlite3_exec(db, sql, 0, 0, &err_msg);/* execute the insert */
if (rc != SQLITE_OK )
{
    /* an error has occurred - report it and close program */
    fprintf(stderr, "SQL error: %s\n", err_msg);
    sqlite3_free(err_msg);
    sqlite3_close(db);
    return 1;
}
```

```
sqlite3_close(db); /* close the database connection */
return 0;
}
```

If you run the preceding program with the **ID=12, name=Pickford, age=48 and occupation = Welder** as earlier and then run it again with an ID=12, name=Rowley,age=34 and occupation=Engineer, you should get "**SQL error: UNIQUE constraint failed: Personnel.Id**" on the screen as you cannot have the same ID for two or more rows.

Selecting Rows

We now have a program, shown in Listing 3-4, which will display a single row whose ID is specified by the user. Similarly to the user-entered INSERT from earlier, the SELECT string is pieced together in the code. In this program, we use "SELECT name, age, occupation FROM Personnel WHERE id = ";. So we use the ID to determine the row we want to select.

Selecting a Row Preset

Listing 3-4. csqlselect_onex2b.c

```
#include <sqlite3.h>
#include <stdio.h>

int callback(void *, int, char **, char **);

int main(void)
{
sqlite3 *db;
char *err_msg = 0;
int rc = sqlite3_open("test.db", &db); /* open the database */

/* Test the result of the 'open' command */
if (rc != SQLITE_OK)
{
        fprintf(stderr, "Cannot open database: %s\n",
        sqlite3_errmsg(db));
```

```
        sqlite3_close(db);
        return 1;
}
int idin,idnew;
```

/* ask the user to enter the ID of the row to be selected */

```
printf("enter current ID \n");
scanf("%d", &idin);
```

/* begin the construction of the SELECT string */

```
char str1[] = "SELECT name, age, occupation FROM Personnel WHERE id = ";

char str4[10];
char str5[] = ";";

printf("idin = %d\n", idin);
sprintf(str4, "%d", idin); /* store the entered id in str4 */

strcat(str1,str4); /* concatenate the ID into str1 above */
strcat(str1,str5); /* semi-colon */

printf("select statement is \n"); /* output string to user */
printf(str1);
printf("\n");
```

/* so, for ID=12 */
/* our completed string in str1 will be :- */

/* SELECT name, age, occupation FROM Personnel WHERE id = 12; */

```
char *sql = str1; /* move the completed string to *sql */
```

/* execute the SELECT */

```
rc = sqlite3_exec(db, sql, callback, 0, &err_msg);
```

/* Test the result of the 'sqlite3_exec' command */

```
if (rc != SQLITE_OK )
{
    /* an error has occurred - report it and close program */
        fprintf(stderr, "Failed to select data\n");
        fprintf(stderr, "SQL error: %s\n", err_msg);
        sqlite3_free(err_msg);
        sqlite3_close(db);
        return 1;
}
sqlite3_close(db);
return 0; /* close the database connection */
}

/* This function is called from sqlite3_exec to print out the data */

int callback(void *NotUsed, int argc, char **argv,
char **azColName)
{
NotUsed = 0;
for (int i = 0; i < argc; i++)
{
    printf("%s = %s\n", azColName[i], argv[i] ? argv[i] : "NULL");
}
printf("\n");

return 0;
}
```

The output if you selected id of 1 would be

```
select statement is
SELECT name, age, occupation FROM Personnel WHERE id = 1;
Name = Brown
Age = 42
Occupation = accountant
```

Selecting All Rows

The following program, shown in Listing 3-5, selects all of the rows in the Personnel table. This is specified by saying 'SELECT *' in the command. The asterisk indicates that all rows are to be selected.

Listing 3-5. csqlselect_allx2b.c

```
#include <sqlite3.h>
#include <stdio.h>
int callback(void *, int, char **, char **);
int main(void)
{
sqlite3 *db;
char *err_msg = 0;
int rc = sqlite3_open("test.db", &db);/* check the database */

if (rc != SQLITE_OK)
{
    /* an error has occurred - report it and close program */
    fprintf(stderr, "Cannot open database: %s\n",
    sqlite3_errmsg(db));
    sqlite3_close(db);
    return 1;
}

/* 'SELECT *'means select everything */

char *sql = "SELECT * FROM Personnel";
rc = sqlite3_exec(db, sql, callback, 0, &err_msg);/*execute the command */

if (rc != SQLITE_OK )
{
    /* an error has occurred - report it and close program */
    fprintf(stderr, "Failed to select data\n");
    fprintf(stderr, "SQL error: %s\n", err_msg);
    sqlite3_free(err_msg);
```

```
    sqlite3_close(db);
    return 1;
}
sqlite3_close(db); /* close the database connection */
return 0;
}

/* This function is called from sqlite3_exec to print out the data */
int callback(void *NotUsed, int argc, char **argv,
char **azColName)
{
NotUsed = 0;
for (int i = 0; i < argc; i++)
{
    printf("%s = %s\n", azColName[i], argv[i] ? argv[i] : "NULL");
}
printf("\n");

return 0;
}
```

The output would be

```
Id = 1
Name = Brown
Age = 42
Occupation = accountant

Id = 2
Name = Jones
Age = 27
Occupation = programmer

Id = 3
Name = White
Age = 30
Occupation = engineer
```

```
Id = 4
Name = Green
Age = 29
Occupation = electrician

Id = 5
Name = Smith
Age = 35
Occupation = manager

Id = 6
Name = Black
Age = 21
Occupation = secretary

Id = 7
Name = Allen
Age = 41
Occupation = cleaner

Id = 8
Name = Stone
Age = 21
Occupation = receptionist

Id = 9
Name = Wells
Age = 50
Occupation = teacher
```

Selecting Rows by Age

The following program selects all of the rows in the Personnel table where the personnel have ages greater than 25. Apart from an extension to the SELECT statement, it is the same code as the previous program. This is shown in Listing 3-6.

Listing 3-6. csqlselect_allx2c.c

```c
#include <sqlite3.h>
#include <stdio.h>
int callback(void *, int, char **, char **);
int main(void)
{
sqlite3 *db;
char *err_msg = 0;
int rc = sqlite3_open("test.db", &db);/* check the database */

if (rc != SQLITE_OK)
{
    /* an error has occurred - report it and close program */
    fprintf(stderr, "Cannot open database: %s\n",
    sqlite3_errmsg(db));
    sqlite3_close(db);
    return 1;
}

/* The following SELECT statement uses "GROUP BY age HAVING" to restrict
   our selection to people with an age greater than 25 */

char *sql = "SELECT * FROM Personnel GROUP BY age HAVING age > 25";
rc = sqlite3_exec(db, sql, callback, 0, &err_msg);/*execute the command */

if (rc != SQLITE_OK )
{
    /* an error has occurred - report it and close program */
    fprintf(stderr, "Failed to select data\n");
    fprintf(stderr, "SQL error: %s\n", err_msg);
    sqlite3_free(err_msg);
    sqlite3_close(db);
    return 1;
}
sqlite3_close(db); /* close the database connection */

return 0;
}
```

```
/* This function is called from sqlite3_exec to print out the data */
int callback(void *NotUsed, int argc, char **argv,
char **azColName)
{
NotUsed = 0;
for (int i = 0; i < argc; i++)
{
    printf("%s = %s\n", azColName[i], argv[i] ?
        argv[i] : "NULL");
}
printf("\n");

return 0;
}
```

The output would be

```
Id = 2
Name = Jones
Age = 27
Occupation = programmer

Id = 4
Name = Green
Age = 29
Occupation = electrician

Id = 3
Name = White
Age = 30
Occupation = engineer

Id = 5
Name = Smith
Age = 35
Occupation = manager
```

```
Id = 7
Name = Allen
Age = 41
Occupation = cleaner

Id = 1
Name = Brown
Age = 42
Occupation = accountant

Id = 9
Name = Wells
Age = 50
Occupation = teacher
```

Amending Rows

In the next program, the user can amend a specified row. The program asks the user if they want to amend the age, name, or occupation. For each of the three options, a separate set of code is written to set up the UPDATE command string. This is shown in Listing 3-7.

Listing 3-7. csqlselect_update11.c

```c
#include <sqlite3.h>
#include <stdio.h>
int main(void)
{
int idin,agenew,optin;
char namenew[13];
char occupnew[15];

sqlite3 *db;
char *err_msg = 0;
sqlite3_stmt *res;
int rc = sqlite3_open("test.db", &db); /* check the database */
```

```
if (rc != SQLITE_OK)
{
    /* an error has occurred - report it and close program */
    fprintf(stderr, "Cannot open database: %s\n",
    sqlite3_errmsg(db));
    sqlite3_close(db);
    return 1;
}
```

/* begin to construct the string */

```
char str3[20];
char str1[80] = "UPDATE Personnel SET ";

char str9[2];
char str15[] = ";";
char str16[] = ", ";
char str17[] = ")";
char str18[] = "\'";

printf("enter id \n");
scanf("%d", &idin);
```

/* The user can amend either age, name or occupation for the specified id for the row. We ask them which they want to amend */

```
    printf("Do you want to update age, name or occupation (1,2 or 3)\n");
    scanf("%d", &optin);
    if(optin == 1)
    {
        /* Amend the age */

        printf("enter new age \n");
        scanf("%d", &agenew);

        strcat(str1," age = "); /* add age */
        strcat(str1,str18);
        sprintf(str3, "%d", agenew); /* copy new age to str3*/
        strcat(str1,str3); /* add new age */
```

```
        strcat(str1,str18); /* add quote */
    }
    else if(optin == 2)
    {
        /* Amend the name */

        printf("enter new name \n");
        scanf("%s", namenew);
        strcat(str1," name = ");
        strcat(str1,str18);
        strcpy(str3, namenew); /* copy new name to str3*/

        strcat(str1,str3); /* add new name */
        strcat(str1,str18); /* add quote */

    }
    else
    {
        /* Amend the occupation */

        printf("enter new occupation \n");
        scanf("%s", occupnew);
        strcat(str1," Occupation = ");
        strcpy(str3,occupnew); /* copy new occupation to str3*/

        strcat(str1,str18); /* add quote */
        strcat(str1,str3); /* add new occupation */
        strcat(str1,str18); /* add quote */
    }
char str2[] = " WHERE id = ";

char str4[6];

strcat(str1,str2); /* copy 'WHERE id = ' string */
sprintf(str4, "%d", idin); /* copy id into str4 */
printf(str4);
strcat(str1,str4); /* copy id into final string */

printf(str1);
```

```
/* so, if we want to update the occupation for ID=12 */
/* our completed string will be :- */
/* UPDATE Personnel SET  Occupation = 'Programmer' WHERE id = 12 */

char *sql = str1;
rc = sqlite3_exec(db, sql, 0, 0, &err_msg); /* perform the insert */
if (rc != SQLITE_OK )
{
    /* an error has occurred - report it and close program */
    fprintf(stderr, "SQL error: %s\n", err_msg);
    sqlite3_free(err_msg);
    sqlite3_close(db);
    return 1;
}
sqlite3_close(db); /* close the database connection */
return 0;

}
```

Deleting Rows

This program, shown in Listing 3-8, deletes a row for the ID specified by the user. You could run the "Selecting All Rows" program, after running this one, to check that the delete has worked.

Listing 3-8. csqlinsert_deletexx.c

```
#include <sqlite3.h>
#include <stdio.h>
int main(void)
{
sqlite3 *db;
char *err_msg = 0;
sqlite3_stmt *res;
int rc = sqlite3_open("test.db", &db); /* check the database */
```

```
if (rc != SQLITE_OK)
{
   /* failure in opening the database file */

   fprintf(stderr, "Cannot open database: %s\n",
       sqlite3_errmsg(db));
   sqlite3_close(db);
   return 1;
}
int idin;
```

/* ask the user to enter the ID if the row to be deleted */

```
printf("enter  id to be deleted\n");
scanf("%d", &idin);
```

/* construct the DELETE string */

```
char str1[200] = "DELETE FROM Personnel WHERE id =   ";
char str2[] = " ); ";
char str3[2];
char str4[6];
char str5[] = ", ";
char str6[] = "'";

sprintf(str4, "%d", idin);

strcat(str1,str4); /* add the entered id to str1 above */
printf(str1); /* print completed string to user */
printf("\n");
```

/* so, if we want to delete the row for ID=12 */
/* our completed string will be :- */

/* DELETE FROM Personnel WHERE id =   12 */

```
   char *sql = str1;
```

```
rc = sqlite3_exec(db, sql, 0, 0, &err_msg); /* perform the delete */
if (rc != SQLITE_OK )
{
    /* an error has occurred - report it and close program */
    fprintf(stderr, "SQL error: %s\n", err_msg);
    sqlite3_free(err_msg);
    sqlite3_close(db);
    return 1;
}
sqlite3_close(db); /* close the database connection */
return 0;

}
```

Summary

This chapter has shown how to insert rows, amend rows, and delete rows from the table.

The chapter shows how we can use the C programming language to implement SQL applications. By doing this, the reader will be able to add SQL database access to their existing C software or create new software which can perform the SQL functions of data table creation and the updating, deleting, and displaying of data.

Exercises

1. Create a program which inserts a number of rows. Ask the user how many rows they want to enter and then create a for loop using this number. Within the for loop, ask the user to enter the data for each row.

2. Using the read file mechanism from Chapter 2, write a program to read in the People3.bin file. Then create a database table and write each record in the file as a row in the table. Then print out the table.

CHAPTER 4

SQL in Python

This chapter introduces the reader to the way the database language, "Structured Query Language," can be accessed and used from a Python program. It will be demonstrated how to create the database file. When this is done, the reader will be able to create database tables. Then, it will be shown how to insert data into the table, how to amend data in the table, how to delete data from the table, and how to print out data held in the table.

Review of SQL

SQL (Structured Query Language) is used to access a database. The easiest way to understand this is to look at an example of a database table. One such table is shown in the following.

A typical database table would contain information about a large number of people working for the same company. The data for one person is contained in a "row." This row holds the person's ID, their surname, their age, and their job title (occupation).

id	surname	initial	gender	age	occupation
123	Jones	A	M	37	Accountant
125	Smith	R	F	42	HR
128	Allen	S	M	28	Secretary
131	Bradley	J	F	26	Programmer
132	Edwards	P	M	41	Programmer
133	King	B	F	35	S/W Engineer
134	Price	C	M	39	H/W Engineer
136	Roberts	M	F	52	Manager

(continued)

© Philip Joyce 2022
P. Joyce, *C and Python Applications*, https://doi.org/10.1007/978-1-4842-7774-4_4

id	surname	initial	gender	age	occupation
138	Foster	M	F	44	Analyst
139	Shannon	M	F	24	Programmer
141	Lewis	R	M	27	Receptionist

We will use **sqlite3** which is a relational database management system. This is in a C library which acts as our interface to SQL.

Create the database from the command line using Python.

Type "Python"

```
>>> import sqlite3
>>> conn = sqlite3.connect('bernard3.db')
```

This creates the database file bernard3.db in the current directory. Its pointer is returned in "conn".

We can use the same name for the database file and one of its tables. So we can call them "Personnel".

We use SQL to create the table. We will call the table "Personnel" so the SQL command for this would be

```
CREATE TABLE Personnel (id INT PRIMARY KEY, surname TEXT, initial TEXT,
gender TEXT, age INT, occupation)
```

In this case, the ID is the "Primary Key" which uniquely identifies the person. So, for example, if two people had the same surname, initial, and gender, then as their ID (primary keys) would be different, this would uniquely identify them.

We would create the row for each person by having a separate "INSERT" statement for each of them. The first person in our table could be defined by the following statement

```
INSERT INTO Personnel  VALUES (123, 'Jones', 'A', 'M', 37, 'Accountant')
```

where 123 is the id, 'Jones' is the surname, 'A' is the initial, 'M' is the gender, 37 is the age, and 'Accountant' is the occupation.

If we wanted the names of all of the programmers in the company, then an SQL statement would say

```
SELECT surname FROM Personnel WHERE occupation = 'Programmer'
```

We can select a specific group using the "HAVING" option, in this case people having an age greater than 25. Here, the "*" in the command means "everybody."

```
SELECT * FROM Personnel GROUP BY age HAVING age > 25
```

We can select a specific group using the "ORDER BY" option.

The following example selects all of the rows from the Personnel table and orders them by age in descending order:

```
SELECT * FROM Personnel ORDER BY age DESC
```

We can amend a row using the "UPDATE" command. The person with id of 123 has their occupation changed to 'manager', as shown as follows:

```
UPDATE Personnel SET  occupation = 'manager' WHERE id = 123
```

Finally, we can delete a row using the "DELETE" command shown here:

```
DELETE FROM Personnel WHERE id = 136;
```

We will use the sqlite3 standard software which is downloadable free of charge.

The Python programs use import sqlite3 which gives the programs access to the sqlite3 library routines.

sqlite3.connect opens the database connection and returns the connection object. So if we have conn = sqlite3.connect('Personnel.db'), we can use conn to access the routines. Here, we then use cur = conn.cursor() to set up cur which will then access, for instance, the execute command shown in the following:

```
cur.execute('CREATE TABLE Personnel (id INTEGER PRIMARY KEY, name TEXT,
initial TEXT, gender TEXT, age INTEGER, occup TEXT)')
```

conn.close() closes the database connection.

Having seen these basic ideas, we can now proceed to write the programs.

Create a Table

This program creates the "Personnel" table as described earlier.

The actual database is the file Personnel.db. Our database tables are added into this.

Listing 4-1 demonstrates this.

Listing 4-1. pycretab.py

```
import sqlite3

conn = sqlite3.connect('Personnel.db') # open connection to database file
Personnel.db
cur = conn.cursor() #open connection to 'cursor' which facilitates SQL
print ("Opened database successfully")

cur.execute('DROP TABLE IF EXISTS Personnel') # delete the table if it
already exists
cur.execute('CREATE TABLE Personnel (id INTEGER PRIMARY KEY, name TEXT,
initial TEXT, gender TEXT, age INTEGER, occup TEXT)') #create the table,
specifying the items in each row

conn.close() # close the database connection
```

The output is

Opened database successfully

Mechanism for Inserting a Row

To insert a row (as described earlier), we set up the "INSERT INTO" command.

In the command "INSERT INTO", when we are executing the command, we have (?, ?, ?, ?, ?, ?) after the VALUES part of the command. In the bracketed section after this, we have the values which will be substituted into the positions of the question marks. So

```
'INSERT INTO Personnel (id, name, initial, gender, age, occup) VALUES (?,
?, ?, ?, ?, ?)',
    (1, 'Jones', 'A', 'M', 23, 'Accountant'))
```

would produce

```
'INSERT INTO Personnel (id, name, initial, gender, age, occup) VALUES (1,
'Jones', 'A', 'M', 23, 'Accountant'))
```

This is a useful mechanism when the user is asked to enter data to be inserted, updated, or deleted where the values in the bracket after VALUES will just be the values entered by the user.

The preceding method "presets" the data into the INSERT command string. Later, we will have programs which allow the user to insert the ID, name, initial, gender, age, and occupation into the program while the program is running.

Create a Table and Insert Two Preset Rows

This program creates the table and inserts two preset rows. Then it selects all of the rows from the table so that we can see the rows inserted. We use the command 'DROP TABLE IF EXISTS Personnel' to make sure that if the table we are trying to create already exists, then it will be deleted. Otherwise, our program would fail with the error "sqlite3. OperationalError: table Personnel already exists". It is shown in Listing 4-2.

Listing 4-2. pycretabins2.py

```
import sqlite3

conn = sqlite3.connect('Personnel.db') # open connection to database file
Personnel.db
cur = conn.cursor()#open connection to 'cursor' which facilitates SQL

print ("Opened database successfully")

cur.execute('DROP TABLE IF EXISTS Personnel') # delete the table if it
already exists

cur.execute('CREATE TABLE Personnel (id INTEGER PRIMARY KEY, name TEXT,
initial TEXT, gender TEXT, age INTEGER, occup TEXT)') #create the table,
specifying the items in each row
# Now Insert two rows into the table

cur.execute('INSERT INTO Personnel (id, name, initial, gender, age, occup)
VALUES (?, ?, ?, ?, ?, ?)',
    (1, 'Jones', 'A', 'M', 23, 'Accountant'))
cur.execute('INSERT INTO Personnel (id, name, initial, gender, age, occup)
VALUES (?, ?, ?, ?, ?, ?)',
    (2, 'Smith', 'J', 'M', 47, 'Salesman'))
```

```
print('Personnel:')
# Select everything contained in the table
cur.execute('SELECT id, name, initial, gender, age, occup FROM Personnel')
for row in cur:
    print(row) # print each row contained in the table

conn.commit() #commit these transaction so they can be seen by other
programs

conn.close() #close the database connection
```

The output is

```
Opened database successfully
Personnel:
(1, 'Jones', 'A', 'M', 23, 'Accountant')
(2, 'Smith', 'J', 'M', 47, 'Salesman')
```

Insert Six Preset Rows

This program, shown in Listing 4-3, inserts six preset rows. If you run this program after the preceding example, then the six rows should be added to the table. Note that we do not create the table in the following program as this would delete the previous two rows inserted. You just insert six separate cur.execute('INSERT INTO Personnel') instructions into the program.

Listing 4-3. pyins6.py

```
import sqlite3

conn = sqlite3.connect('Personnel.db') # open connection to database file
Personnel.db
cur = conn.cursor()#open connection to 'cursor' which facilitates SQL

print ("Opened database successfully")

# Now Insert six rows into the table

cur.execute('INSERT INTO Personnel (id, name, initial, gender, age, occup)
VALUES (?, ?, ?, ?, ?, ?)',
    (11, 'Jones', 'A', 'M', 23, 'Accountant'))
```

```
cur.execute('INSERT INTO Personnel (id, name, initial, gender, age, occup)
VALUES (?, ?, ?, ?, ?, ?)',
    (12, 'Smith', 'J', 'M', 47, 'Salesman'))
cur.execute('INSERT INTO Personnel (id, name, initial, gender, age, occup)
VALUES (?, ?, ?, ?, ?, ?)',
    (13, 'Zeiss', 'H', 'F', 38, 'Architect'))
cur.execute('INSERT INTO Personnel (id, name, initial, gender, age, occup)
VALUES (?, ?, ?, ?, ?, ?)',
    (14, 'Blaine', 'S', 'F', 28, 'SE'))
cur.execute('INSERT INTO Personnel (id, name, initial, gender, age, occup)
VALUES (?, ?, ?, ?, ?, ?)',
    (15, 'Postlethwaite', 'D', 'M', 63, 'Advisor'))
cur.execute('INSERT INTO Personnel (id, name, initial, gender, age, occup)
VALUES (?, ?, ?, ?, ?, ?)',
    (16, 'Junkers', 'A', 'M', 59, 'Designer'))
print('Personnel:')
cur.execute('SELECT id, name, initial, gender, age, occup FROM Personnel')
# Select everything contained in the table

for row in cur:
    print(row) # print each row contained in the table

conn.commit()#commit these transaction so they can be seen by other
programs
conn.close() #close the database connection
```

The output is

```
Opened database successfully
People:
(1, 'Jones', 'A', 'M', 23, 'Accountant')
(2, 'Smith', 'J', 'M', 47, 'Salesman')
(11, 'Jones', 'A', 'M', 23, 'Accountant')
(12, 'Smith', 'J', 'M', 47, 'Salesman')
(13, 'Zeiss', 'H', 'F', 38, 'Architect')
(14, 'Blaine', 'S', 'F', 28, 'SE')
(15, 'Postlethwaite', 'D', 'M', 63, 'Advisor')
(16, 'Junkers', 'A', 'M', 59, 'Designer')
```

Insert a Row Specified by the User

Now that we have our database table with its rows, we may want to add another row (if, say, the company has just recruited a new employee).

We now have a program which will insert a single row whose ID and their other fields are specified by the user. The program asks the user to insert each field in turn. It is shown in Listing 4-4.

Listing 4-4. pyuserins1.py

```
#!/usr/bin/python

import sqlite3

conn = sqlite3.connect('Personnel.db') # open connection to database file
Personnel.db
cur = conn.cursor()#open connection to 'cursor' which facilitates SQL
print ("Opened database successfully")
# User is asked to enter the name, ID, initial, gender, age and occupation

while True:
    namein = input('Enter an name, or quit: ') # age stored in namein

    if(namein == 'quit'): break   #exit the while loop
    idin = input('Enter ID: ') # id stored in 'idin'
    initial = input('Enter initial: ') # initial stored in 'initial'
    gender = input('Enter gender: ') # gender stored in 'gender'
    agein = input('Enter age: ') # age stored in 'agein'
    occup = input('Enter occupation: ') # occupation stored in 'occup'

# Now Insert row into the table using the values entered

    cur.execute('INSERT INTO Personnel (id, name, initial, gender, age,
    occup) VALUES (?, ?, ?, ?, ?, ?)',(idin, namein, initial, gender,
    agein, occup))
    break

print('Personnel:')
# Select everything contained in the table
```

```
cur.execute('SELECT id, name, initial, gender, age, occup FROM Personnel')
for row in cur:
    print(row) # print each row contained in the table
```

`conn.commit()`**#commit these transaction so they can be seen by other programs**

`conn.close()`**#close the database connection**

If we type the following

Enter an name, or quit: Robinson
Enter ID: 21
Enter initial: C
Enter gender: F
Enter age: 31
Enter occupation: Engineer

we get

Personnel:
(1, 'Jones', 'A', 'M', 23, 'Accountant')
(2, 'Smith', 'J', 'M', 47, 'Salesman')
(11, 'Jones', 'A', 'M', 23, 'Accountant')
(12, 'Smith', 'J', 'M', 47, 'Salesman')
(13, 'Zeiss', 'H', 'F', 38, 'Architect')
(14, 'Blaine', 'S', 'F', 28, 'SE')
(15, 'Postlethwaite', 'D', 'M', 63, 'Advisor')
(16, 'Junkers', 'A', 'M', 59, 'Designer')
(21, 'Robinson', 'C', 'F', 31, 'Engineer')

Update a Row

Update a Row, Preset

In this program, shown in Listing 4-5, we update a row in the table, for instance, if we wanted to change their age or job title. The values to be updated are coded into the program. We use the UPDATE command and say SET to say which item in the row we wish to change. It is safest to use the ID to specify which row we wish to change. In the example here, we have used the name to specify the row, but, as you may notice, because there are two people in the table with the same name, it has updated both of the rows.

Listing 4-5. pyup1.py

```
import sqlite3

conn = sqlite3.connect('Personnel.db') # open connection to database file
Personnel.db

cur = conn.cursor()#open connection to 'cursor' which facilitates SQL
# Now update the row in the table
# we want to set the age for the person named Smith to be 24

try:
                cur.execute("UPDATE Personnel SET age = 24 WHERE name =
                'Smith'")
 except Error as e:
                print(e)
# Select everything contained in the table

cur.execute("SELECT * FROM Personnel")
cur.execute('SELECT id, name, initial, gender, age, occup FROM Personnel')
for row in cur:
    print(row)

conn.commit()#commit these transaction so they can be seen by other
programs
cur.close()
```

The output is

```
(1, 'Jones', 'A', 'M', 23, 'Accountant')
(2, 'Smith', 'J', 'M', 24, 'Salesman')
(11, 'Jones', 'A', 'M', 23, 'Accountant')
(12, 'Smith', 'J', 'M', 24, 'Salesman')
(13, 'Zeiss', 'H', 'F', 38, 'Architect')
(14, 'Blaine', 'S', 'F', 28, 'SE')
```

```
(15, 'Postlethwaite', 'D', 'M', 63, 'Advisor')
(16, 'Junkers', 'A', 'M', 59, 'Designer')
(21, 'Robinson', 'C', 'F', 31, 'Engineer')
```

Notice that, here, we have two people named Smith, so the UPDATE has changed both of the rows. This is the type of thing you need to beware of. Here, the safest way would be to use the ID rather than the name.

Update a Row by User

In this program, shown in Listing 4-6, we update a row in the table. The values to be updated are entered by the user to update the age.

The program uses the function conn.total_changes which returns total changes to the table since connection. So, if there is only one change made (INSERT, UPDATE, or DELETE) and the function conn.total_changes returns zero, then we know that the attempted change must have failed.

Listing 4-6. pyuserup1.py

```
import sqlite3

conn = sqlite3.connect('Personnel.db') # open connection to database file
Personnel.db
cur = conn.cursor()#open connection to 'cursor' which facilitates SQL
# we want to set the age for the person whose name is entered into 'namein'
to be the age which is entered into 'agein'

#the following is a while loop which can only be exited by the user
entering "quit".
while True:
    namein = input('Enter an name, or quit: ')
    if(namein == 'quit'): break
    print(namein)
    agein = input('Enter age: ')

    # Using a while loop
    tot0 = 0
# Now update the row in the table
```

```
try:

    cur.execute("UPDATE Personnel SET age = ? WHERE name = ?",
    (agein,namein,))

except:
    print('Error in Update')

#conn.total_changes returns total changes since connection
# by setting tot0 to 0 before this update then only this
# update is checked
tot = conn.total_changes
print(tot)
if tot == tot0:
    print('Table not updated')
else
# Select everything contained in the table

    cur.execute('SELECT id, name, initial, gender, age, occup FROM
    Personnel')
    for row in cur:
            print(row)

conn.commit()#commit these transaction so they can be seen by other
programs

cur.close()#close the database connection
```

The output is (assuming we enter Junkers for the name and 38 for age)

```
(1, 'Jones', 'A', 'M', 23, 'Accountant')
(2, 'Smith', 'J', 'M', 24, 'Salesman')
(11, 'Jones', 'A', 'M', 23, 'Accountant')
(12, 'Smith', 'J', 'M', 24, 'Salesman')
(13, 'Zeiss', 'H', 'F', 38, 'Architect')
(14, 'Blaine', 'S', 'F', 44, 'SE')
(15, 'Postlethwaite', 'D', 'M', 63, 'Advisor')
(16, 'Junkers', 'A', 'M', 38, 'Designer')
(21, 'Robinson', 'C', 'F', 31, 'Engineer')
Enter a name, or quit:
```

142

Insert and Update a Row

We can do an insert and an update in the same program. In this case, both the insert and the update are preset in the code. This is shown in Listing 4-7.

Listing 4-7. pyinsup.py

```
import sqlite3

conn = sqlite3.connect('Personnel.db') # open connection to database file
Personnel.db

cur = conn.cursor()#open connection to 'cursor' which facilitates SQL
#insert the row, specifying the items in the row
cur.execute('INSERT INTO Personnel (id, name, initial, gender, age, occup)
VALUES (?, ?, ?, ?, ?, ?)',
    (25, 'Van der Kirchoff', 'I', 'M', 34, 'plumber'))
#update a different row, specifying the changed item in the row

    cur.execute("UPDATE Personnel SET age = 28 WHERE name = 'Smith'")
# Select everything contained in the table

    cur.execute("SELECT * FROM Personnel ")
    # print each row contained in the table

    cur.execute('SELECT id, name, initial, gender, age, occup FROM
    Personnel')
  for row in cur:
    print(row)

conn.commit()#commit these transaction so they can be seen by other
programs

cur.close()#close the database connection
```

The output is

```
(1, 'Jones', 'A', 'M', 23, 'Accountant')
(2, 'Smith', 'J', 'M', 28, 'Salesman')
(11, 'Jones', 'A', 'M', 23, 'Accountant')
(12, 'Smith', 'J', 'M', 28, 'Salesman')
```

```
(13, 'Zeiss', 'H', 'F', 38, 'Architect')
(14, 'Blaine', 'S', 'F', 28, 'SE')
(15, 'Postlethwaite', 'D', 'M', 63, 'Advisor')
(16, 'Junkers', 'A', 'M', 37, 'Designer')
(21, 'Robinson', 'C', 'F', 31, 'Engineer')
(25, 'Van der Kirchoff', 'I', 'M', 34, 'plumber')
```

Select a Row

In this program, we select a row from the table. The values to be used in the selection are coded into the program. We use the SELECT command and the WHERE instruction to specify which row we are interested in. The command to select by age would be

```
SELECT * FROM Personnel  WHERE age = 28
```

The program follows in Listing 4-8.

Listing 4-8. pysel1.py

```
import sqlite3

conn = sqlite3.connect('Personnel.db') # open connection to database file
Personnel.db
cur = conn.cursor()#open connection to 'cursor' which facilitates SQL

# Select one row contained in the table where the age is 28
# If we did not have LIMIT 1 then every row which had an age of 28 would be
displayed

cur.execute("SELECT * FROM Personnel  WHERE age = 28 LIMIT 1")
#print the row selected

for row in cur:
    print(row)

conn.commit()#commit these transaction so they can be seen by other
programs

cur.close()#close the database connection
```

The output is

```
(2, 'Smith', 'J', 'M', 28, 'Salesman')
```

Select a User-Entered Row

In this program, shown in Listing 4-9, we select a row from the table. The values to be used in the selection are entered by the user. The user wants to find the age of the person named. This is displayed when found.

Listing 4-9. pyusersel1.py

```
import sqlite3

conn = sqlite3.connect('Personnel.db') # open connection to database file
Personnel.db
cur = conn.cursor()#open connection to 'cursor' which facilitates SQL

while True:
    namein = input('Enter an name, or quit: ')
    if(namein == 'quit'): break
    print(namein)

    cur.execute('SELECT age FROM Personnel WHERE name = ? LIMIT 1',
    (namein, ))

    (age, ) = cur.fetchone()
    print(age)
    break
conn.commit()#commit these transaction so they can be seen by other
programs

cur.close()#close the database connection
```

The output is (if we enter the name "Zeiss")

```
Enter an name, or quit: Zeiss
Zeiss
38
```

Select by Age in Descending Order

Select all of the rows in the table by age and order in descending order of age. This is done within the SQL select statement

```
SELECT * FROM Personnel ORDER BY age DESC
```

This will order the whole table in descending order of age. Listing 4-10 shows the code.

Listing 4-10. pyselorder.py

```
import sqlite3

conn = sqlite3.connect('Personnel.db') # open connection to database file
Personnel.db
cur = conn.cursor()#open connection to 'cursor' which facilitates SQL

cur.execute("SELECT * FROM Personnel ORDER BY age DESC")
for row in cur:
    print(row)

conn.commit()#commit these transaction so they can be seen by other
programs

cur.close()#close the database connection
```

The output is

```
(15, 'Postlethwaite', 'D', 'M', 63, 'Advisor')
(13, 'Zeiss', 'H', 'F', 38, 'Architect')
(16, 'Junkers', 'A', 'M', 37, 'Designer')
(25, 'Van der Kirchoff', 'I', 'M', 34, 'plumber')
(21, 'Robinson', 'C', 'F', 31, 'Engineer')
(14, 'Blaine', 'S', 'F', 28, 'SE')
(2, 'Smith', 'J', 'M', 24, 'Salesman')
(12, 'Smith', 'J', 'M', 24, 'Salesman')
(1, 'Jones', 'A', 'M', 23, 'Accountant')
(11, 'Jones', 'A', 'M', 23, 'Accountant')
```

User-Entered Select by Age

This program, shown in Listing 4-11, selects people from the table whose ages are greater than the value the user specifies. This is done using "HAVING" as in the SELECT command

```
("SELECT * FROM Personnel GROUP BY age HAVING age > ?",(ageins,))
```

where "ageins" is the age specified by the user.

Listing 4-11. pyusersel1hav.py (user inputs age)

```
import sqlite3

conn = sqlite3.connect('Personnel.db') # open connection to database file
Personnel.db
cur = conn.cursor()#open connection to 'cursor' which facilitates SQL

ageins = input('Enter age: ')

print(ageins)

while True:

    # Using a while loop

    cur.execute("SELECT * FROM Personnel GROUP BY age HAVING age > ?",
    (ageins,))

        for row in cur:
         print(row)
    break
conn.commit()#commit these transaction so they can be seen by other
programs

cur.close()#close the database connection
```

If you enter 24, the output is

```
(14, 'Blaine', 'S', 'F', 28, 'SE')
(21, 'Robinson', 'C', 'F', 31, 'Engineer')
(25, 'Van der Kirchoff', 'I', 'M', 34, 'plumber')
```

147

```
(16, 'Junkers', 'A', 'M', 37, 'Designer')
(13, 'Zeiss', 'H', 'F', 38, 'Architect')
(15, 'Postlethwaite', 'D', 'M', 63, 'Advisor')
```

Delete a Row

This program, shown in Listing 4-12, deletes a row from the table. The user enters the name of the person whose row is to be deleted. You could run the "Read a Table" program, from the next section, after the "Delete a Row" program to check that it has worked.

Listing 4-12. pydel1.py

```
import sqlite3

conn = sqlite3.connect('Personnel.db') # open connection to database file
Personnel.db
cur = conn.cursor()#open connection to 'cursor' which facilitates SQL
print ("Opened database successfully")

namein = input('Enter an name, or quit: ')

cur.execute('DELETE FROM Personnel WHERE name = ?',(namein,))

print('Personnel:')
cur.execute('SELECT id, name, initial, gender, age, occup FROM Personnel')
for row in cur:
     print(row)

conn.commit()#commit these transaction so they can be seen by other
programs

conn.close()#close the database connection

user enters Blaine
```

The output is

```
Personnel:
(1, 'Jones', 'A', 'M', 23, 'Accountant')
(2, 'Smith', 'J', 'M', 24, 'Salesman')
(11, 'Jones', 'A', 'M', 23, 'Accountant')
```

```
(12, 'Smith', 'J', 'M', 24, 'Salesman')
(13, 'Zeiss', 'H', 'F', 38, 'Architect')
(15, 'Postlethwaite', 'D', 'M', 63, 'Advisor')
(16, 'Junkers', 'A', 'M', 38, 'Designer')
(21, 'Robinson', 'C', 'F', 31, 'Engineer')
 (25, 'Van der Kirchoff', 'I', 'M', 34, 'plumber')
```

Read a Table

This program, shown in Listing 4-13, reads and prints out all of the rows in the table. The lines of code which do this could be used in any of the other programs in this chapter. So if you have made any amendments or inserted or deleted any rows, the user can check if the changes have worked.

Listing 4-13. pyreadtab.py

```
import sqlite3

conn = sqlite3.connect('Personnel.db') # open connection to database
file Personnel.db cur = conn.cursor()#open connection to 'cursor' which
facilitates SQL
print ("Opened database successfully")
cur = conn.cursor()#open connection to 'cursor' which facilitates SQL

print(' Personnel:')
cur.execute('SELECT id, name, initial, gender, age, occup FROM Personnel')
for row in cur:
    print(row)

conn.commit()#commit these transaction so they can be seen by other
programs
conn.close()#close the database connection
```

The output is

```
Opened database successfully
People:
(1, 'Jones', 'A', 'M', 23, 'Accountant')
(2, 'Smith', 'J', 'M', 24, 'Salesman')
```

```
(11, 'Jones', 'A', 'M', 23, 'Accountant')
(12, 'Smith', 'J', 'M', 24, 'Salesman')
(13, 'Zeiss', 'H', 'F', 38, 'Architect')
(15, 'Postlethwaite', 'D', 'M', 63, 'Advisor')
(16, 'Junkers', 'A', 'M', 37, 'Designer')
(21, 'Robinson', 'C', 'F', 31, 'Engineer')
(25, 'Van der Kirchoff', 'I', 'M', 34, 'plumber')
```

Summary

This chapter has demonstrated how to use the Python programming language to create SQL database tables and then to insert, amend, and delete rows in the table. It has also shown how to display the data in the table in different specific orders. This will enable users to adapt their existing programs to include SQL access or to write new Python programs for SQL applications.

Exercises

1. Create two tables whose SQL equivalent is as follows:

   CREATE TABLE Personnel (id INTEGER, name TEXT, initial, gender TEXT, age INTEGER, occup TEXT)

   and

   CREATE TABLE supply (id INTEGER, coname TEXT, address TEXT, type TEXT)

   Then insert six rows into the first table and four into the second table. The second table is a list of companies. The name of the company is supplied in "coname", and the type of goods they supply is in "type".

2. Amend the insert program, **pyuserins1.py**, so that you can insert as many rows into the table as you want.

CHAPTER 5

Embedded Python

The C programming language has been in operation since the early 1970s and has been central to the development of computer software since then. The Python language is newer and can perform some functions that C does not. So, it is useful to be able to write a C program and have some Python code incorporated (embedded) into it. This is what this chapter will illustrate.

We'll look at the following two levels of Python code that can be incorporated into a C program:

- Call a simple Python string.

- Call a Python program.

To embed the two levels into our C program, we have to initialize the Python interpreter. The main function call is Py_Initialize(). At the end of the Python sequence, we call Py_Finalize();.

To call a simple string, we use PyRun_SimpleString.

To run a Python program, we use `PyRun_SimpleFile`.

Python has matplotlib and numpy which can be embedded into C programs. These will be introduced in the sections where the program uses them.

The listings will be labeled as "Listing 5-1", etc., and the associated embedded Python program will be labeled with an extension of "b". So here, its label would be "Listing 5-1b".

Basic Mechanism

Listing 5-1 demonstrates the simple string option described earlier. The Python just prints 'Embedded Python string'.

© Philip Joyce 2022
P. Joyce, *C and Python Applications*, https://doi.org/10.1007/978-1-4842-7774-4_5

Listing 5-1. cpyth1.c

```c
#include <stdio.h>
#include "include/Python.h"
int main()
{
    Py_Initialize();
    PyRun_SimpleString("print('Embedded Python string')");
    Py_Finalize();
    return 0;
}
```

This program prints

Embedded Python string

Listing 5-2 demonstrates the second embedding option. Here, we call the Python program pyemb7.py. We create a variable called char filename[] which will hold the filename to be called. We define the variable fp which is the file pointer.

Listing 5-2. cpyth8.c

```c
#define PY_SSIZE_T_CLEAN
#include <stdio.h>
#include <conio.h>
#include "include/Python.h"

int main()
{
    char filename[] = "pyemb7.py"; /* store the python file name */
    FILE* fp; /* file pointer */

    Py_Initialize();

    fp = _Py_fopen(filename, "r"); /* store file pointer in fp */
    PyRun_SimpleFile(fp, filename);/* call the python program */

    Py_Finalize(); /* end the python link */
    return 0;
}
```

The following Listing 5-2b is the simple Python program which is called.

Listing 5-2b. pyemb7.py

```
print('Embedded Python program here')
print('Hello to C program')
```

This program prints

Embedded Python program here
Hello to C program

We can now progress to a more realistic Python embedding.

Plot a 2D Line

The next C program is basically the same as the previous one, except that it calls a different Python program. Listing 5-3 demonstrates this.

Listing 5-3. cpyth17a.c

```c
#define PY_SSIZE_T_CLEAN
#include <stdio.h>
#include <conio.h>
#include "include/Python.h"

int main()
{
    char filename[] = "plot6a.py";
    FILE* fp;

    Py_Initialize();

    fp = _Py_fopen(filename, "r");
    PyRun_SimpleFile(fp, filename);

    Py_Finalize();
    return 0;
}
```

This Python program (Listing 5-3b) demonstrates the use of numpy and matplotlib. Numpy is a numerical set of procedures, and matplotlib is concerned with plotting graphs. The Python program plots the straight line y = x + 3. We set our x values using the numpy function np.arange(0,10). This creates x values between 0 and 10 evenly spaced. We calculate the y value for each of these x values using y = x + 3.

We then call the matplotlib function plt.plot(x,y) to plot the graph.

Listing 5-3b. plot6a.py

```python
import numpy as np
from matplotlib import pyplot as plt

x = np.arange(0,10) #return evenly spaced values between 0 and 10
y = x + 3 # formula to calculate y values for the x values given in the
previous instruction
plt.title("Embedded ")  #title of graph
plt.xlabel("x axis") #x axis label
plt.ylabel("y axis") #y axis label
plt.plot(x,y) #plot the graph
plt.show()
```

This produces the graph shown in Figure 5-1.

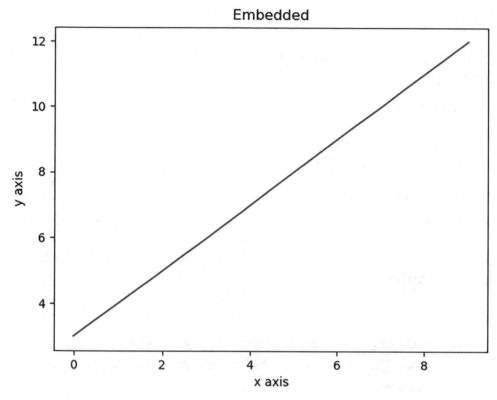

Figure 5-1. *Basic straight line of y = x + 3*

We can now move to plotting two lines on a graph.

Plot Two 2D Lines

This combination of C and Python shows some of the flexibility of matplotlib in Python. It plots two curves on the same graph. Listing 5-4 demonstrates this.

Listing 5-4. cpyth29.c

```
#define PY_SSIZE_T_CLEAN
#include <stdio.h>
#include <conio.h>
#include "include/Python.h"
```

```
int main()
{
    char filename[] = "mp2aa.py";
    FILE* fp;

    Py_Initialize();

    fp = _Py_fopen(filename, "r");
    PyRun_SimpleFile(fp, filename);

    Py_Finalize();
    return 0;
}
```

Listing 5-4b. mp2aa.py

-

This program (Listing 5-4b) plots two graphs. One graph shows the distribution of examination marks (in percent values) for females, and the other graph shows the distribution of examination marks for males.

We use the **list(range(0,100,10))** function to create a set of x values (the marks) for both graphs.

```
import matplotlib.pyplot as plt
# x values:
marks = list(range(0,100,10)) #marks (x values) in range 0 to 100 in units
of 10
# y values:
male = [4, 7, 9, 17, 22, 25, 28, 18, 6, 2] # number of males within each
range
female = [2, 5, 8, 13, 28, 25, 23, 20, 18, 12] # number of females within
each range

# x axis label and y axis label
plt.xlabel('marks')
plt.ylabel('number of students')

#title of graph
plt.title('Comparison of male / female examination scores')
```

```
#plot points and adjoining lines for both male and female
#show a key to which line is male and which is female
plt.plot(marks, female, label="female")
plt.plot(marks, female, "ob")  # ob means plot a circle character which is
blue
plt.plot(marks, male, label="male")
plt.plot(marks, male, "or") # or means plot a circle character which is red

plt.legend()
plt.show()
```

This program plots the curves shown in Figure 5-2.

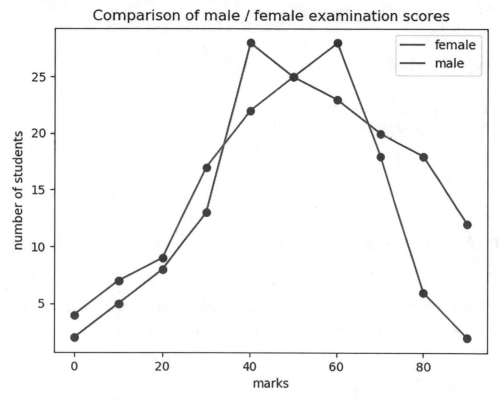

Figure 5-2. *Comparison of male-female examination marks*

The two graphs show a similar distribution for both male and female students. This general shape is called the "Normal Distribution."

Matplotlib can also plot standard trigonometric curves as shown in the following.

Plot Trigonometric Curves

This next combination in Listing 5-5 shows the standard matplotlib tan(x) function.

Listing 5-5. cpyth32.c

```
#define PY_SSIZE_T_CLEAN
#include <stdio.h>
#include <conio.h>
#include "include/Python.h"

int main()
{
    char filename[] = "mp5ae.py";
    FILE* fp;

    Py_Initialize();

    fp = _Py_fopen(filename, "r");
    PyRun_SimpleFile(fp, filename);

    Py_Finalize();
    return 0;
}
```

Listing 5-5b. mp5ae.py

-

In this program (Listing 5-5b), we use np.arange(-2*np.pi, 2*np.pi, 0.1) to give us a set of x values which are multiples of pi. Thus, we can plot a standard trigonometric function.

```
import numpy as np
import matplotlib.pyplot as plt

# Choose evenly spaced x intervals
x = np.arange(-2*np.pi, 2*np.pi, 0.1)

# plot y = tan(x)
plt.plot(x, np.tan(x))
```

```
# Set the range of the axes
plt.axis([-2*np.pi, 2*np.pi, -2, 2])

# Include a title
plt.title('y = tan(x)')

# Optional grid-lines
plt.grid()
plt.xlabel('x values')
plt.ylabel('y values')
# Show the graph
plt.show()
```

This program plots the curve shown in Figure 5-3.

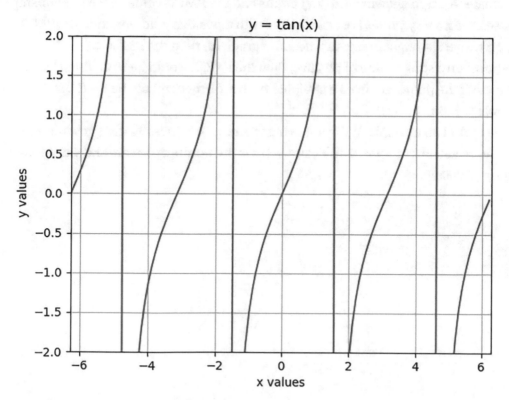

Figure 5-3. *Standard curve of y = tan(x)*

The grid plot is a matplotlib option. In the case of tan trigonometric curve, it is useful to include the grid as it shows the asymptotic lines.

We can allow the user to enter data points to be plotted as shown in the next example.

Enter Data to Plot

The next example has a more significant C program. The program calculates the mathematical value Product Moment Correlation Coefficient. This is a measure of the relationship between x and y values in a graph. The user enters the x and y values. The C program calculates the PMCC for these values and writes this to the file `pmccfcnt.bin` and the x and y values to the file `pmccf.bin`. The Python program reads these two files and creates a graph showing the (x,y) points and the PMCC value. If the relationship between the x and y values is a straight line with a positive gradient, then the PMCC is +1. If we get a straight line with a negative gradient, then the PMCC is –1. If the points are almost on a straight line of positive, then the PMCC would be something like 0.9568. The further the points are from a straight line, the further will be the PMCC from 1, for example, 0.7453.

We look at an example in the following where we are investigating how the value of a car depreciates over 6 years. In Figure 5-4, x is the number of years and y is the car's value in $1000s.

Data for car depreciation (8 points)

x	y
2.5	11.5
3.0	10.6
3.5	9.2
4.0	7.8
4.5	6.1
5.0	4.7
5.5	3.9
6.0	1.8

Figure 5-4. *x,y points for car depreciation*

The graph of this is shown in Figure 5-5.

Value ($1000)

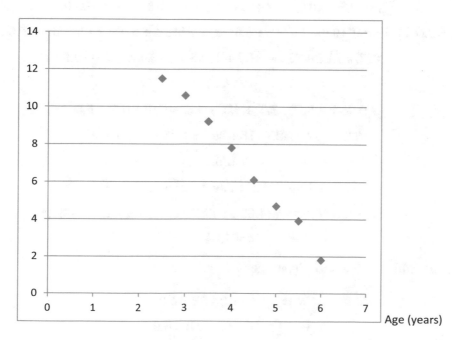

Figure 5-5. *Car depreciation graph*

PMCC for car depreciation is 0.996961.

The formula for the PMCC, **r**, is

$$r = S_{xy} / (S_x \cdot S_y) \qquad (1)$$

$$\text{where } S_x = \sqrt{S_{xx}} \qquad (2)$$

$$\text{and } S_y = \sqrt{S_{yy}} \qquad (3)$$

$$S_{xx} = \sum x^2 - (\sum x)^2 / n \qquad (4)$$

$$S_{yy} = \sum y^2 - (\sum y)^2 / n \qquad (5)$$

$$S_{xy} = \sum xy - (\sum x \sum y) / n \qquad (6)$$

$\sum$**x** means sum all of the x values.

$\sum$**y** means sum all of the y values.

$\sum$**x²** means square all of the x values and then sum them.

$\sum$**y²** means square all of the y values and then sum them.

$\sum$**xy** means multiply each x,y pair and then sum them.

Using these values in our six formulas, we get

$$\sum x = 2.5 + 3.0 + 3.5 + 4.0 + 4.5 + 5.0 + 5.5 + 6.0 = 34$$

$$\sum y = 11.5 + 10.6 + 9.2 + 7.8 + 6.1 + 4.7 + 3.9 + 1.8 = 55.6$$

$$\sum xy = 2.5*11.5 + 3.0*10.6 + 3.5*9.2 + 4.0*7.8 + 4.5*6.1 + 5.0*4.7 + 5.5*3.9 + 6.0*1.8$$

$$= 28.75 + 31.8 + 32.2 + 31.2 + 27.45 + 23.5 + 21.45 + 10.8$$

$$= 207.15$$

$$\sum x^2 = 2.5^2 + 3.0^2 + 3.5^2 + 4.0^2 + 4.5^2 + 5.0^2 + 5.5^2 + 6.0^2$$

$$= 6.25 + 9 + 12.25 + 16 + 20.25 + 25 + 30.25 + 36$$

$$= 155$$

$$\sum y^2 = 11.5^2 + 10.6^2 + 9.2^2 + 7.8^2 + 6.1^2 + 4.7^2 + 3.9^2 + 1.8^2$$

$$= 132.25 + 112.36 + 84.64 + 60.84 + 37.21 + 22.09 + 15.21 + 3.24$$

$$= 467.84$$

From our values of $\sum$x and $\sum$y, we get

$$\bar{x} = \sum x / 8 = 34 / 8 = 4.25$$

$$\bar{y} = \sum y / 8 = 55.6 / 8 = 6.95$$

From our values of $\sum x^2$, $\sum y^2$, and $\sum xy$, we get

$$S_{xx} = \sum x^2 - (\sum x)^2 / n$$
$$= 155 - 34^2 / 8 = 10.5$$
$$S_{yy} = \sum y^2 - (\sum y)^2 / n$$
$$= 467.84 - 55.6^2 / 8 = 81.42$$
$$S_{xy} = \sum xy - (\sum x \sum y) / n$$
$$= 207.15 - 34*55.6 / 8 = -29.15$$

So we can now write

$$S_x = \sqrt{S_{xx}} = 3.24037$$
$$S_y = \sqrt{S_{yy}} = 9.0233$$

Using these values for PMCC

$$r = S_{xy} / (S_x * S_y)$$
$$= -29.15 / (3.24037 * 9.0233)$$
$$= -0.996961$$

So our value for the Product Moment Correlation Coefficient for the car depreciation problem is –0.996961. This is very close to –1 which would be perfect negative correlation.

If you are not familiar with the preceding terms, $\sum$ is the Greek letter "sigma." So in the following program, we call $\sum x$ "sigmax" and similarly for the other terms used earlier.

In the program, we use sigmax, sigmay, sigmaxsquared, sigmaysquared, xbar, ybar, sigmaxy;.

In the following program, shown in Listing 5-6, the user is asked to enter the data points in x,y pairs. When you run this program, enter the following points:

```
x values    y values

1.000000    2.000000
2.000000    3.000000
3.000000    5.000000
4.000000    9.000000
5.000000    10.000000
6.000000    13.000000
```

Listing 5-6. pmccf3.c

```c
/*product moment correlation coefficient */
#define _CRT_SECURE_NO_WARNINGS
#define PY_SSIZE_T_CLEAN
#include <stdio.h>
#include <math.h>
#include <conio.h>
#include "include/Python.h"

main()
{
    double xpoints[10], ypoints[10];
    double sigmax, sigmay, sigmaxsquared, sigmaysquared, xbar, ybar,
    sigmaxy;
    double sxy, sxx, syy, sx, sy, r;
    int i, points;
    double fltcnt;
char filename[] = "searchpj3b.py"; /* python program to be called */
    FILE* fp2;

    FILE *fp;
        FILE *fp3;

    fp=fopen("pmccf2.bin","w"); /* file to store (x,y) values */
    fp3=fopen("pmccfcnt2.bin","w"); /* file to PMCC value */

    /* User enters number of points in scatter graph */
    /* with a maximum of 10 */

    printf("enter number of points (max 10 ) \n");
    scanf("%d", &points);
    if (points > 10)
    {
        /* User set number of points to be greater than 10 */
        /* Flag an error */

        printf("error - max of 10 points\n");

    }
```

```
else
{
    fprintf(fp3,"%d\n",points);

    /* set store areas to zero */
    sigmax = 0;
    sigmay = 0;
    sigmaxy = 0;
    sigmaxsquared = 0;
    sigmaysquared = 0;

    /* User enters points for scatter graph */
    for (i = 0;i < points;i++)
    {
        printf("enter point (x and y separated by space) \n");
        scanf("%lf %lf", &xpoints[i], &ypoints[i]);
        /* totals incremented by x and y points */
        sigmax = sigmax + xpoints[i];
        sigmay = sigmay + ypoints[i];
        sigmaxy = sigmaxy + xpoints[i] * ypoints[i];
        sigmaxsquared = sigmaxsquared + pow(xpoints[i], 2);
        sigmaysquared = sigmaysquared + pow(ypoints[i], 2);
    }

    /*print points and write them to file */

    printf("points are \n");
    for (i = 0;i < points;i++)
    {
        printf(" \n");
        printf("%lf %lf", xpoints[i], ypoints[i]);
        fprintf(fp,"%lf\t%lf\n",xpoints[i], ypoints[i]);
    }
    printf(" \n");
    fltcnt = points;
```

```c
/* variables in PMCC formula calculated */

xbar = sigmax / fltcnt;
ybar = sigmay / fltcnt;

syy = (1 / fltcnt)*sigmaysquared - ybar * ybar;

sxx = (1 / fltcnt)*sigmaxsquared - xbar * xbar;
sx = sqrt(sxx);
sy = sqrt(syy);
sxy = (1 / fltcnt)*sigmaxy - xbar * ybar;

/* PMCC value calculated */

r = sxy / (sx*sy);
printf("r is %lf", r);
fprintf(fp3,"%lf\n",r);
}
fclose(fp);

fclose(fp3);

/* Call python program to print the graph */

 Py_Initialize();

fp2 = _Py_fopen(filename, "r");
PyRun_SimpleFile(fp2, filename);

Py_Finalize();

}
```

The Python program (Listing 5-6b) reads the file of data and creates the graph.

Listing 5-6b. searchpj3b.py

```python
import matplotlib.pyplot as plt
import numpy as np

#if there are 8 entered coordinates then this will be the arrays
#xvals = [0,1,2,3,4,5,6,7]
```

```
#yvals = [0,1,2,3,4,5,6,7]
#xvals = [0]*8
#yvals = [0]*8

# Read data from pmccf.bin file

y = np.loadtxt("pmccf.bin")
print("Data read from pmccf.bin")
print("y = ",y)

# Read data from pmccfcnt.bin file

z = np.loadtxt("pmccfcnt.bin")
print("Data read from pmccfcnt.bin")
print("z = ",z)
a,b = z # a is no. of coords entered, b is PMCC value

#zint is the number of coordinates entered
zint = int(a)
print("number of coordinates entered = ", zint)

print("PMCC = ", b)
float_b = b;
string_b = str(float_b)

# Set up the arrays for the graph

xvals = [0]*zint #length of array is num. of coords entered
yvals = [0]*zint #length of array is num. of coords entered

# set up the x and y arrays from the values entered
for x in range(zint):
    a,b = y[x]
    xvals[x] = a
    yvals[x] = b

# Print the x and y values to the user

print("xvals = ",xvals)
print("yvals = ",yvals)
```

Display the graph

```
plt.xlabel('x values')
plt.ylabel('y values')
plt.title('PMCC Test Graph')
plt.text(1.0, 10, 'PMCC =')
plt.text(2.0, 10, string_b)

plt.plot(xvals, yvals, "ob")
plt.show()
```

This outputs to the command lines

```
enter number of points (max 10 )
6
enter point (x and y separated by space)
1 2
enter point (x and y separated by space)
2 3
enter point (x and y separated by space)
3 5
enter point (x and y separated by space)
4 9
enter point (x and y separated by space)
5 10
enter point (x and y separated by space)
6 13
points are

1.000000 2.000000
2.000000 3.000000
3.000000 5.000000
4.000000 9.000000
5.000000 10.000000
6.000000 13.000000
r is 0.986227
Data read from pmccf.bin
```

```
y =  [[ 1.  2.]
 [ 2.  3.]
 [ 3.  5.]
 [ 4.  9.]
 [ 5. 10.]
 [ 6. 13.]]
Data read from pmccfcnt.bin
z =  [6.        0.986227]
number of coordinates entered =  6
PMCC =  0.986227
xvals =  [1.0, 2.0, 3.0, 4.0, 5.0, 6.0]
yvals =  [2.0, 3.0, 5.0, 9.0, 10.0, 13.0]
```

This produces the graph shown in Figure 5-6.

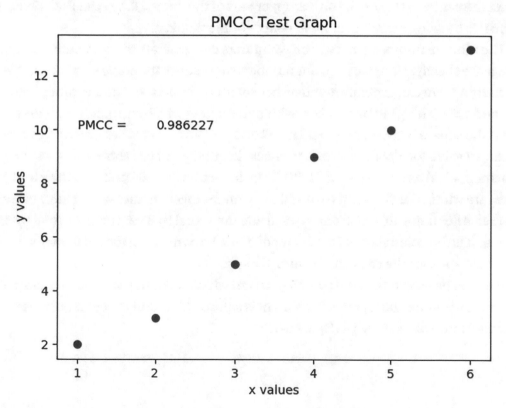

Figure 5-6. *PMCC test graph*

In this case, the calculated PMCC is 0.986227 which is very close to +1 which would be perfect positive correlation where all of the points would lie exactly on a straight line.

Next, we will look at a mechanism for finding the center of mass of an object.

2D Center of Mass Plot

Here, we want to find where the center of mass of the area enclosed by the 2D U-shaped curve (y = x**2) and the line y = 4 lies. If you made a shape as in Figure 5-7 and you made it a solid shape from wood or plaster of Paris and then held the shape flat, you should be able to balance it on your finger by placing your finger below the center of mass point.

If you look at the following diagram, you can see that it is symmetrical about the line x = 0 so that you would expect the center of mass to lie on that line. Also, looking at the object, you can see that there is more matter in the top part of the shape so you would expect the center of mass to be on the upper part of the line x = 0. We can find out exactly where it is by using a random number generator mechanism.

The random number generator on computers can generate random numbers within a range we specify. Here, we want our numbers to be above the curve y = x**2 and below the line y = 4. We can generate numbers between x = –2 and x = +2 and y values between y = 0 and y = 4. This gives us numbers within the square which surrounds our curve. This is the square between x = –2 and x = +2 and y =0 and y = 4. When we have generated an x and y value for a point, we need to check that that point lies above the curve or, in mathematical terms, that y > x**2. We keep doing this for 3500 points. If the x and y values are within the curve, then we add the x values together and we add the y values together. After doing this 3500 times, we divide the x total by 3500 and the y total by 3500. The result is the coordinates of the center of mass. We write all of the 3500 points to an output file and also the calculated center of mass.

We then pass control to the Python program which reads the two files and plots all of the points generated on a graph. Each point is colored blue, and the center of mass point is colored red. This is shown in Figure 5-7.

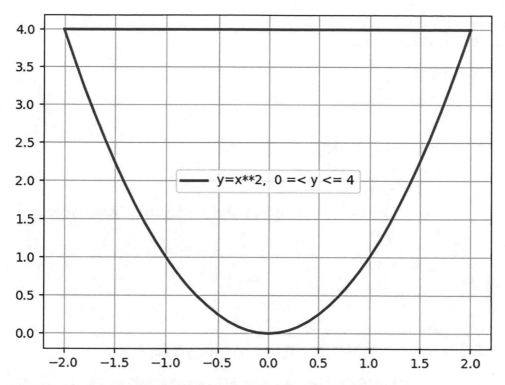

Figure 5-7. *Shape whose center of mass we want to find*

The C program is cofm5a.c (Listing 5-7), and the embedded Python program is searchpj4.py (listing 5-7b).

Listing 5-7. cofm5a.c

```
/*      cofm5a.c
    Centre of Mass Calculation.
In this program "Centre of Mass" is abbreviated to cofm.
    Calculates c of m for 2D shape y = x^^2 between y = 0 and y = 4 */
#define _CRT_SECURE_NO_WARNINGS
#define PY_SSIZE_T_CLEAN
#include <stdlib.h>
#include <stdio.h>
#include <math.h>
#include <time.h>
```

```
#include <conio.h>
#include "include/Python.h"

double randfunc();
main()
{

        int   I,outcount;
        float area,total,count;
        FILE *fptr;
        char filename[] = "searchpj4.py"; /* python program name */
        FILE* fp2;

        FILE *fp3;

        time_t t;

        /*  Local Arrays */
   double x, y,xout[3500],yout[3500],xcofm,ycofm;

        /* file cofm5a.bin contains all points inside the curve */
        /* file cofm5acnt.bin contains total number of points inside
            the curve and the x and y position of the centre of mass*/

        fptr=fopen("cofm5a.bin","w");
        fp3=fopen("cofm5acnt.bin","w");

        /* Initializes random number generator */
        srand((unsigned) time(&t));

        /* clears arrays to zero */
     for( I = 0;  I<3500;I++)
        {
                xout[I] = 0.0;
                yout[I] = 0.0;

        }
```

```
        /* set x and y cofm accumulators to zero */
        xcofm=0.0;
        ycofm=0.0;

        total = 0.0;
        count = 0.0;
        outcount = 0;
for( I = 1;I<= 3500;I++)
{
                /* get x values between -2 and +2 */
                /* get y values between 0 and +4 */
        x = randfunc()*4.0-2.0;
        y = randfunc()*4.0;

                /* If the generated x and y values are above */
                /* the curve y=x^2 then add 1 to count */
                /* and update the x and y cofm values */

        if(y>pow(x,2))
        {
                xcofm=xcofm+x;
                ycofm=ycofm+y;

                total = total+1;
                outcount = outcount +1;
                xout[outcount] = x;
                yout[outcount] = y;
        }
        count = count+1;

}

        area=(total/count)*16;/* area is part of the square which is
        4x4 or 16 sq units */
        printf("total is %f count is %f\n",total,count);

        xcofm=xcofm/total;
        ycofm=ycofm/total;
```

```
            printf("area is %lf\n",area);
            printf("cofm is %lf,%lf",xcofm,ycofm);

            /*  Plot the data */

            if(outcount >= 2700)
                    outcount = 2700;

            fprintf(fp3,"%d\t%lf\t%lf\n",outcount,xcofm,ycofm);

        for(I = 1; I<=outcount-1;I++)
                    fprintf(fptr,"%lf %lf\n",xout[I],yout[I]);
            fclose(fptr);
fclose(fp3);

/* Call python program to read the file and produce the diagram showing the
position of the centre of mass */

Py_Initialize();

            fp2 = _Py_fopen(filename, "r");
            PyRun_SimpleFile(fp2, filename);

            Py_Finalize();

}

double randfunc()
{

            /* get a random number 0 to 1 */
            double ans;

            ans=rand()%1000;
            ans=ans/1000;

            return ans; /* return the random number to the caller */

}
```

Listing 5-7b. searchpj4.py

```python
#In this program "Centre of Mass" is abbreviated to cofm.

import matplotlib.pyplot as plt
import numpy as np
fhand = open('cofm5a.bin','r') #file of (x,y) values created by Cofm5a.c

count = 0
#if there are 8 entered coordinates then this will be the arrays
#xvals = [0,1,2,3,4,5,6,7]
#yvals = [0,1,2,3,4,5,6,7]
#xvals = [0]*8
#yvals = [0]*8

y = np.loadtxt("cofm5a.bin") # read x,y values
print("Data read from cofm5a.bin")
print(y)

z = np.loadtxt("cofm5acnt.bin") # read count of points, xcofm and ycofm
print("Data read from cofm5acnt.bin")
print(z)
a,p,j = z # split the 3 z values into separate variables
zint = int(a)
print("zint is " ,zint) # total number of points
string_p = str(p)
print("string_p is ",string_p ) # x value of c of m
string_j = str(j)
print("string_j is ",string_j ) # y value of c of m

xvals = [0]*zint
yvals = [0]*zint
# store the x and y coordinates into xvals[] and yvals[]
for x in range(zint-1):
    a,b = y[x]
    xvals[x] = a
    yvals[x] = b
```

```
plt.xlabel('x values')
plt.ylabel('y values')
plt.title(' CofM Graph (red spot is Centre of Mass)')
plt.plot(xvals, yvals, "ob")
plt.plot(p, j, "or")
plt.show()
```

This code produces the following output to the command line:

```
total is 2331.000000 count is 3500.000000
area is 10.656000
cofm is 0.006847,2.359818Data read from cofm5a.bin
[[-1.548  3.268]
 [-0.872  2.716]
 [-0.16   0.068]
 ...
 [ 0.136  2.972]
 [ 0.18   0.172]
 [ 1.484  3.744]]
Data read from cofm5acnt.bin
[2.331000e+03 6.847000e-03 2.359818e+00]
zint is  2331
string_p is  0.006847
string_j is  2.359818
```

This code produces the following graph shown in Figure 5-8.

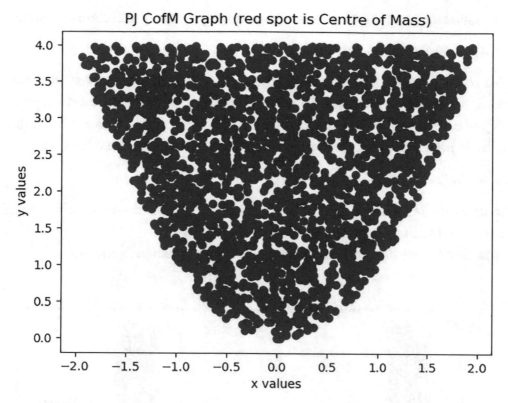

Figure 5-8. *Center of mass graph*

The center of mass is shown by the red spot. You could guess that this is probably correct as the shape of the object is symmetrical about the line x = 0 and the spot looks to be on that line, and there are more blue dots in the top of the shape and the red spot is toward the top of the shape.

This embedded Python program demonstrates the advantages of both C and Python and so the usefulness of the embedding technique.

We will now look at histograms as they are useful in many areas of economics.

Histograms

A histogram is a graphical way of representing data distributions. They are similar to bar charts in appearance, but they show frequency density as a distribution rather than frequency.

The bars in the graphs are referred to as "bins."

The following program shows a histogram displaying the distribution of numbers:

`1,2,3,4,45,66,67,68,69,70,84.88,91,94`

The program takes these values and groups them into ten bins. We specify in the program that we want ten bins, and this value is used in the call to the function plt.hist which plots the histogram. The reply from the call to this function tells you how many items are in each bin. We can then print this out, and we see that the values are

4. 0. 0. 0. 1. 0. 1. 4. 0. 3.

So there are four items in the first bin (1,2,3,4 from our list of values earlier), none in the next three bins, one in the next, etc.

In Listing 5-8, we then plot the histogram which is shown in Figure 5-9.

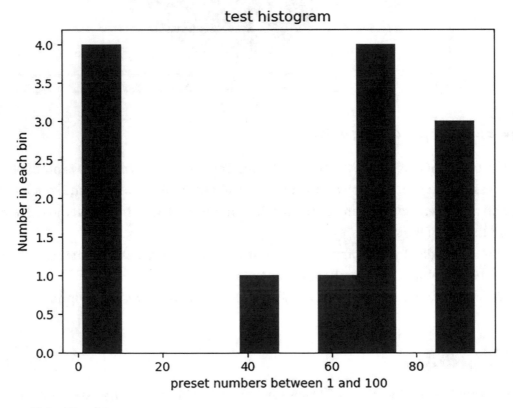

Figure 5-9. *Test histogram*

Listing 5-8. plot2b.py

```
import matplotlib.pyplot as plt

values = [1,2,3,4,45,66,67,68,69,70,84.88,91,94]
# draw a histogram with 10 bins of the `values' data

number_of_bins = 10

n = plt.hist(values, number_of_bins, facecolor='blue')

print(n[0]) # counts in each bin

# plot the histogram

plt.title('test histogram')
plt.xlabel('preset numbers between 1 and 100')
plt.ylabel('Number in each bin')
plt.show()
```

This outputs

```
[4. 0. 0. 0. 1. 0. 1. 4. 0. 3.]
```

This histogram mechanism is used in the exercise at the end of the chapter. Our final example shows how we can import a picture into our program.

Importing a Picture

Python has "Image", "ImageDraw", and "ImageFont" which can be imported from "PIL" and embedded into C programs. These can be used by a Python program to read a photographic image in a file and print it. We can then overwrite some of the pictures with text. Listing 5-9 demonstrates this.

Listing 5-9. cpythim1.c

```
#define PY_SSIZE_T_CLEAN
#include <stdio.h>
#include <conio.h>
#include "include/Python.h"
```

```c
int main()
{
    char filename[] = "embim9.py";
    FILE* fp;

    Py_Initialize();

    fp = _Py_fopen(filename, "r");
    PyRun_SimpleFile(fp, filename);

    Py_Finalize();
    return 0;
}
```

The Python program (Listing 5-9b) reads a file containing a picture of Rome and draws the image. It then writes a title "Rome 2016" at the top of the image. This is shown in Figure 5-10.

Figure 5-10. *Imported picture*

Listing 5-9b. embim9.py

```
from PIL import Image, ImageDraw, ImageFont
#Open image using Image module
im = Image.open("5Rome.jpg") #photograph of Rome

myFont = ImageFont.truetype(r'C:\Users\System-Pc\Desktop\arial.ttf', 80)
#The 'r' character before the path, in the code above, is necessary if the
path contains backslashes, #as the backslash could be interpreted as an
escape character.
d1 = ImageDraw.Draw(im)
# Print text "Rome 2016" at the top of the picture
d1.text((28, 36), "Rome 2016", font=myFont, fill=(255, 0, 0))

#Show final Image
im.show()
```

Summary

This chapter has demonstrated how you can embed Python code and complete Python programs into C programs. We have shown how this can be invaluable if you need to perform tasks which Python is more able to do than C.

Exercise

1. Write a C program to read in 20 user-entered marks achieved by students in an examination (0 to 100). Write the 20 marks to a file. Write a Python program to read the file, and from the 20 values, create a histogram. Call the Python program from the C program.

CHAPTER 6

Sockets

The socket system allows two or more programs to communicate with each other over the Internet. Messages can be sent between the programs in both directions, if required. Files can be transmitted, and we can have one socket communicating with several others at the same time (this is called "multithreading").

A Closer Look at Sockets

The term for two sockets communicating using predefined sequences is called "handshaking." These predefined sequences are called "protocols." Both server and client have to adhere to the same protocols; otherwise, they would not work. This is a bit like two people who spoke different languages and neither knew the other person's language. Their communication would break down fairly quickly.

One fairly well-used protocol is TCP/IP which is an abbreviation of "Transmission Control Protocol/Internet Protocol." This protocol is used over the Internet. Each device which uses the Internet has its own "IP address." This is a unique address. You can find the IP address of the computer you use using the command-line tool "ipconfig". IP addresses have the same format. One address may be "123.456.7.89". The addresses always have the same pattern of four numbers separated by a full stop (period). This type of IP address is called IPv4, and the address is 32 bit. There is a new version of IP addressing called IPv6, where the address is 128 bit. Here we will use IPv4.

The socket system in Python is accessed using our familiar "**import**" instruction. In this case, we use

```
import socket
```

Programs that use the socket system are classed as either "**server**" or "**client**." Generally speaking, the server is in charge of the communication, and the client asks to be connected to it. Once the connection has been established, messages can be sent from server to client and from client to server.

© Philip Joyce 2022

P. Joyce, *C and Python Applications*, https://doi.org/10.1007/978-1-4842-7774-4_6

Figure 6-1 shows the main code calls from a server and a client.

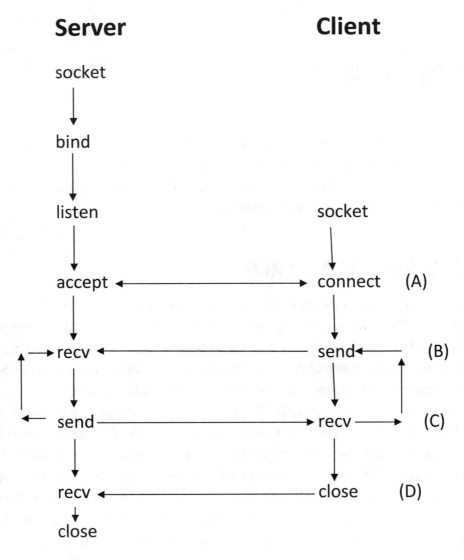

Server sets itself up as a listening socket

(A)   Connection between server and client

(B)   Data sent from client to server

(C)   Data sent from server to client

(D)   Client closes connection

Figure 6-1. *Server-client mechanism*

On each side, the program issues the "**socket**" command which initiates the socket mechanism in the program.

On the server side, the next command is "**bind**". This establishes the program that issues the "bind" as a server. The IP address and port number are given in the bind command.

The next command for the server is "**listen**". Here, the server waits for connect commands from client programs.

On the client side, after the initial "**socket**" command, it issues a "**connect**" command to make a connection with the server. It then calls "**connect**" to connect to the specific server (identified by IP address and port number).

The server now issues an "**accept**" command to accept the connect command from the client.

Now that the connection has been established, the server and client can send and receive messages to and from each other.

When all business between the server and client is complete, the client sends a "**close**" command to the server and the connection between them is ended.

Messages sent across the Internet normally use UTF-8.

UTF-8 is part of Unicode which is an international standard for giving every character a unique number. It is similar to ASCII. It uses either 1, 2, 3, or 4 bytes to encode (usually only 1 byte).

The data in the messages is normally in string format, and this is translated into UTF-8 using the .encode() command. If the server program sends this to the client program, then the client translates this back into string format using .decode().

We can now look at different types of socket.

Basic Client-Server

This is a basic one-way, server and client combination. There is a basic connection and communication, as described in the preceding diagram. The server starts up and waits for a connection from the client. The client starts up and connects to the server. The server sends a message to the client. The client receives this message and prints it. Then the connection terminates.

If your client and server are on the same machine, then you can use the command "gethostname" to get its identifier and then use this with its port number for its full address. If your server and client are on different machines, then you cannot use "gethostame", but you have to use their IP addresses.

Here, our server and client are on the same machine, so we can use "gethostame". If we want to find our IP address, we can use the command socket. gethostbyname(hostname).

Listing 6-1 is the server.

Listing 6-1. socser10cx.py

```
# socket server

import socket                 # load socket module

skt = socket.socket()             # Create a socket (refer to it as skt in this
                                  program)
hostname = socket.gethostname()  # Get local host machine name
print(hostname)  #print the host machine name
port = 12357                   # Reserve a port (same as client port)
skt.bind((hostname, port))       # Bind the host name and port (establish
                                       server status)

skt.listen(5)                   # wait for a client to connect.
while True:
    con, accaddr = skt.accept()      # Accept connection with client.
                                     # 'con' is the open connection between
                                       the server and client,  'accaddr' is
                                       the IP address and port number
    print('con is ', con) #print values to the user
    print('accaddr is ', accaddr) #print values to the user

    print('Received connection from', accaddr) #print values to the user

    message = "Got your connection"
    con.send(message.encode()) #send message to client to confirm connect

    con.close()                 # Close connection
    break
```

The server outputs the following:

user-PC

con is   <socket.socket fd=448, family=AddressFamily.AF_INET, type=SocketKind.SOCK_STREAM, proto=0, laddr=('123.456.7.89, 12357), raddr=(123.456.7.89', 63730)>

accaddr is   ('123.456.7.89', 63730)

Received connection from ('123.456.7.89', 63730)

(where the "123.456.7.89" characters are the IP addresses).

The second program, Listing 6-2, is the client.

Listing 6-2. soccli10bx.py

 # socket client

```
import socket              # load socket module

skt = socket.socket()          # Create a socket
hostname = socket.gethostname() # Get local machine name
port = 12357               # Reserve a port (must be same as server)

skt.connect((hostname, port)) # connect to the server
data = skt.recv(1024) # receive data from server
            print('data is ',data.decode()) #print the line of data
                                         received
skt.close()               # Close connection
```

The client outputs the following:

data is Got your connection

This has shown a basic socket operation. We will now look at file transfer between sockets.

Server-Client Pair to Send-Receive a File

The following server-client pair send/receive a file.

The server reads each line of the file "pjfile1.txt" and sends each one separately to the client.

"pjfile1.txt" contains

```
This is my line
second line
third line
fourth line
last line
```

The client reads each line received from the server, prints it out, and writes it to the output file "pjrecfile".

Listing 6-3 shows the server for a file send.

Listing 6-3. socserfile.py

```
# send file to client

import socket                  # Import socket module

port = 3000                    # Reserve a port for your service.
s = socket.socket()            # Create a socket object
host = socket.gethostname()    # Get local machine name
s.bind((host, port))           # Bind to the port
s.listen(5)                    # Now wait for client connection.

print ('Server running')

while True:
    conn, addr = s.accept()    # Establish connection with client.
    print ('Got connection from', addr)
    data = conn.recv(1024) #receive connection from client
    print('Server received', bytes.decode(data)) #print out the data
                                                  received

    filename='pjfile1.txt'  #the name of the file to be opened
    file = open(filename,'rb') #open the file we wish to send
# read each line in the file and send it to the client
line = file.read(1024)
    while (line):
        conn.send(line) #send the line to the client
```

```
    print('Server received ',bytes.decode(line)) #tell user the line
                                                  that has been received
                                                  by client

      line = file.read(1024) #read the next line
    file.close() #finished sending so close the file

    print('Finished sending')
    conn.send(str.encode('Thank you for connecting')) #send final message
                                                      to client

    conn.close() #close the connection
    break
```

After connecting, the server outputs

Server received Client connected
Sent   This is my line
second line
third line
fourth line
last line

Finished sending

The next program, shown in Listing 6-4, is the associated client program which reads and prints the file. It then creates an output file and writes the file read to it.

Listing 6-4. socclifile.py

```
# Socket Client Program
# receive file from server
# and write it to a new file

import socket                    # Import socket module

s = socket.socket()             # Create a socket object
host = socket.gethostname()     # Get local machine name
port = 3000                     # Set the port for your service.

s.connect((host, port)) # connect to server
s.send(str.encode("Client connected")) #send connect confirmation to user
```

```
# open the output file (pjrecfile)
with open('pjrecfile', 'wb') as file:
    print ('file opened')
    while True:
        print('receiving data from server')
        data = s.recv(1024) # receive each line of data from server (at
                            most 1024 bytes)
        print('data is ',bytes.decode(data)) #print the line of data
                            received

        if not data:
            break
        # write data to the file
        file.write(data)

file.close() # close the output file
print('Received file from server')
print('Written to output file pjrecfile')
s.close() #close the connection
print('connection closed')
```

After connecting, the client outputs

file opened
receiving data from server
data is This is my line
second line
third line
fourth line
last line

receiving data from server
data is Thank you for connecting
receiving data from server
data is
Received file from server
Written to output file pjrecfile
connection closed

pjrecfile contains

```
This is my line
second line
third line
fourth line
last line
Thank you for connecting
```

This has shown a method of file transfer with sockets. Until now, we have only looked at one server communicating with one client. We will now extend this.

Threaded Programs

A threaded system of sockets can have a few client programs connecting simultaneously to one server. Clients can connect and disconnect as many times as they wish. The server sits in a loop waiting for client connections. Listing 6-5 shows the code for the threaded server.

Listing 6-5. socserthreadgx2.py

```python
import socket      # Import socket module
from _thread import * # thread software
import os

mypid = os.getpid()# get Process ID (pid)for this program
print('Server My pid is', mypid) #print the pid in case the user wants to
                                 'taskkill' this program

ServerSocket = socket.socket()
host = socket.gethostname()      # Get local machine name

port = 1234
ThreadCount = 0     #count of how many clients have connected
ServerSocket.bind((host, port))

print('Waiting for Client connect')
ServerSocket.listen(5) #wait for a client connection
```

```
# Function for each connected client
def threadcli (cliconn):
    cliconn.sendall(str.encode('Connect'))
    while True:
        data = cliconn.recv(2048) #receive message from client
        reply = 'Server replies: ' + data.decode() #set up reply
        if not data:
            break
        cliconn.sendall(str.encode(reply)) #send the reply to the client
    cliconn.close()

# wait for a connection from a new client
while True:
    Cli, addr = ServerSocket.accept()
    print('Connected to: ' + addr [0] + ':' + str(addr [1]))
    print(Cli) # show server and client addresses
    start_new_thread(threadcli, (Cli, )) #function imported from  '_thread'
                             # This calls local function 'threadcli'
                             # Each threaded client stays within its own
                             # 'threadcli' function
        ThreadCount += 1 #add 1 to number of connected clients
    print('Thread Number: ' + str(ThreadCount))
ServerSocket.close()
```

After connecting, the server outputs

Server My pid is 6296
Waiting for Client connection
Connected to: ....(IP address and Port
number)
Thread Number: 1

The second program is the client. When the client wants to end the connection, the user types in 'windup' and the connection is closed. Listing 6-6 shows the code for the threaded client.

Listing 6-6. socclithreadgx2.py

```python
import socket
import os

mypid = os.getpid() # get Process ID (pid)for this program
print('Client My pid is', mypid) #print the pid

ClientSocket = socket.socket()
host = socket.gethostname()        # Get local machine name

port = 1234

print('Waiting for connection')
ClientSocket.connect((host, port)) #connect to Server

Response = ClientSocket.recv(1024)
print(ClientSocket) # show server and client addresses
while True:
    Input = input('Enter message: ') #ask user to enter their message
    ClientSocket.send(str.encode(Input)) #send message to socket
    Response = ClientSocket.recv(1024) #get response from server

    if( Response.decode()) =='Server replies: windup':
        # if client wants to disconnect from server, the user types
        'windup'
        break
    print(Response.decode())
ClientSocket.close() #close the client
```

After connecting, the client outputs

```
Client My pid is 2248
Waiting for connection
Enter message: hello from client1
Server replies: hello from client1
Enter message: windup
```

This has shown multiple clients connecting to a single server. As clients can connect, disconnect, and then reconnect, this could cause a problem with redundant servers. We will now look at this.

Closing Down a Threaded Server

Most socket clients and servers can be routinely shut down. However, in the case of threaded sockets, the server may be left running indefinitely because many clients can connect and disconnect over a period of time.

If we are sure that all of the clients have disconnected from the server and we want to close the server, we can by using the command-line instructions "tasklist" and "taskkill".

The "tasklist" command provides us with a list of the currently running tasks. An example is shown as follows:

```
C:\Users\user\AppData\Local\Programs\Python\Python37>tasklist
Image Name                     PID Session Name        Session#    Memory Usage
========================= ======== ================ =========== ============
System Idle Process              0 Services                  0            8 K
System                           4 Services                  0           36 K
Registry                       100 Services                  0       51,384 K
smss.exe                       352 Services                  0          648 K
csrss.exe                      516 Services                  0        2,744 K
wininit.exe                    628 Services                  0        3,852 K
services.exe                   700 Services                  0        6,616 K
lsass.exe                      708 Services                  0       14,688 K
svchost.exe                    904 Services                  0       22,944 K
fontdrvhost.exe                932 Services                  0        1,568 K
svchost.exe                     68 Services                  0       14,284 K
cmd.exe                      12004 Console                   3        5,044 K
conhost.exe                   9936 Console                   3       19,564 K
UserOOBEBroker.exe           11604 Console                   3        9,040 K
notepad.exe                   1448 Console                   3       44,144 K
notepad.exe                  10452 Console                   3       41,768 K
python.exe                    6576 Console                   3       10,596 K
cmd.exe                       7104 Console                   3        5,048 K
conhost.exe                   1332 Console                   3       19,580 K
```

cmd.exe	10344 Console	3	5,284 K
conhost.exe	6120 Console	3	19,512 K
Microsoft.Photos.exe	772 Console	3	8,356 K
RuntimeBroker.exe	12072 Console	3	31,176 K
tasklist.exe	4944 Console	3	9,836 K

`C:\Users\user\AppData\Local\Programs\Python\Python37>`

We see that our python.exe program is in this list. We can close this down using "taskkill" as shown as follows:

`C:\Users\user\AppData\Local\Programs\Python\Python37> taskkill /F /IM`
`python.exe`

`SUCCESS: The process "python.exe" with PID 6576 has been terminated.`

`C:\Users\user\AppData\Local\Programs\Python\Python37>`

`OR WE CAN USE THE PID TO TERMINATE IT'`

If there is more than one python.exe running, we need to make sure that we are terminating the correct one. Each running program has a unique Process ID or PID. We can use the pid to make sure we terminate the correct one. Here, we show a task list with two python.exe programs.

`C:\Users\user\AppData\Local\Programs\Python\Python37>tasklist`

Image Name	PID	Session Name	Session#	Memory Usage
System Idle Process	0	Services	0	8 K
System	4	Services	0	36 K
Registry	100	Services	0	52,328 K
smss.exe	352	Services	0	648 K
csrss.exe	516	Services	0	2,752 K
wininit.exe	628	Services	0	3,852 K
services.exe	700	Services	0	6,600 K
lsass.exe	708	Services	0	14,768 K
svchost.exe	904	Services	0	22,944 K
fontdrvhost.exe	932	Services	0	1,568 K
svchost.exe	68	Services	0	14,268 K

svchost.exe	1056 Services	0	19,188 K
svchost.exe	1084 Services	0	25,116 K
svchost.exe	1120 Services	0	23,404 K
svchost.exe	1288 Services	0	27,984 K
svchost.exe	1344 Services	0	66,208 K
notepad.exe	1448 Console	3	44,144 K
notepad.exe	10452 Console	3	41,800 K
cmd.exe	7104 Console	3	5,052 K
conhost.exe	1332 Console	3	19,620 K
cmd.exe	10344 Console	3	5,284 K
conhost.exe	6120 Console	3	19,956 K
Microsoft.Photos.exe	772 Console	3	8,356 K
RuntimeBroker.exe	12072 Console	3	31,196 K
svchost.exe	12704 Services	0	9,592 K
audiodg.exe	4716 Services	0	11,748 K
smartscreen.exe	12000 Console	3	22,928 K
python.exe	5492 Console	3	10,548 K
python.exe	16648 Console	6	11,100 K
tasklist.exe	2448 Console	3	9,824 K

If we know that it is the one with pid of 5492, we can type

C:\Users\user\AppData\Local\Programs\Python\Python37>taskkill /F /PID 5492

and receive

SUCCESS: The process with PID 5492 has been terminated.

C:\Users\user\AppData\Local\Programs\Python\Python37>

If you had two or more python.exe programs running (each having a different pid), you may not know which one to kill. What we can do, if we know that we may want to kill our process from the command line, is for the program in question to print out its pid on startup. It can find its pid using the getpid() Python instruction which is contained in the os library.

So in our program, we would include

```
import os
mypid = os.getpid()
print('My pid is', mypid)
```

So the instruction os.getpid() would return the programs pid in the variable "mypid", and then the program would print this out. The user can then use the "taskkill" command as earlier using the relevant pid, for example:

```
C:\Users\user\AppData\Local\Programs\Python\Python37>python Socclithreadg.py
My pid is 4120
Waiting for connection
<socket.socket fd=420, family=AddressFamily.AF_INET, type=SocketKind.SOCK_
STREAM, proto=0, laddr=('123.456.7.89'), raddr=('123.456.7.89')>
Enter message:
```

Then on a different window, we would use taskkill

```
C:\Users\user\AppData\Local\Programs\Python\Python37>taskkill /F /pid 4120 /T
```

and receive

```
SUCCESS: The process with PID 4120 (child process of PID 16520) has been
terminated.
```

```
C:\Users\user\AppData\Local\Programs\Python\Python37>
```

This section has shown how to close a server. This mechanism should only be used when necessary. We will now look at "chat" programs.

Chat Programs

Chat socket programs have sends and receives in both directions. The server still initiates the connection procedure, but the conversation is two-way (hence "chat").

The first program, shown in Listing 6-7, is the server.

Listing 6-7. socsert2x.py

```
# Server Side Script
# Socket Server Program

import time, socket, sys

server_port = 1000

server_socket = socket.socket()
```

```
host_name = socket.gethostname()
server_socket.bind((host_name ,server_port))

server_socket.listen(1) #look for client connect
print ("Server is loaded")
connection_socket, address = server_socket.accept() # accept client connect
while True:
    sentence = connection_socket.recv(2048).decode() #receive incoming
                                                       message
    print('>> ',sentence) # print the message to the user
    message = input(">> ") #ask the user to input a reply
    connection_socket.send(message.encode()) #send reply
    if(message == 'windup'):
        connection_socket.close() # a 'windup' message means the user wants
                                    to disconnect
        break
```

Output from server (check the client output to see the two-way chat):

Server is loaded
>>   hello from client
>> hello from server
>>   windup
>> windup

The second program, shown in Listing 6-8, is the client. When the client wants to end the chat, the user types in 'windup' and the chat is closed.

Listing 6-8. socclit2x.py

```
# Client Side Script
# Socket Client Program

import time, socket, sys

server_name = socket.gethostname()
server_port = 1000

client_socket = socket.socket()
```

```
host_name = socket.gethostname()

client_socket.connect((server_name,server_port)) #connect to the server
while True:
    sentence = input(">> ") #input your message
    client_socket.send(sentence.encode())#send your message
    message = client_socket.recv(2048) #receive reply
    print (">> ", message.decode()) #print the reply
    if(sentence == 'windup'):
        client_socket.close() # a 'windup' command means the user wants to
                                            disconnect
    break
```

Output from client (check the server output to see the two-way chat):

```
>> hello from client
>>  hello from server
>> windup
>>  windup
```

This has demonstrated two-way send and receive sockets.

The chapter has shown the fundamentals of sockets and the variety of types of communication we can use sockets for.

Summary

This chapter has illustrated how socket servers and clients interact and how they can be used in different combinations.

Exercise

1. Write chat programs for a server and a client. Then write another two where the only difference from the first two is the port number. Run all four programs on different windows. Check that the server-client pair with the same port number chat with each other (i.e., the server with one port number should not chat with the client with a different port number).

APPENDIX A

Answers to Examples

Chapter 1

1.

We get

```
print(type(V1))
```
<class 'int'>
```
print(type(V2))
```
<class 'float'>
```
print(type(V3))
```
<class 'float'>
```
print(type(V4))
```
<class 'float'>

Now we perform arithmetic processes as we did with our int assignments.

```
V5 = V1 + V2
print(V5)
```
5.5
```
print(V1+V2)
```
5.5
```
print(type(V5))
```
<class 'float'>

```
V5 = V4 - V3
print(V5)
```
1.6500000000000004

P. Joyce, *C and Python Applications*, https://doi.org/10.1007/978-1-4842-7774-4

```
V5 = V2 *V1
print(g)
```
7.0

```
V5 = V4 / V1
print(V5)
```
3.375

```
V5 = V2 / V4
print(V5)
```
0.5185185185185185

```
V5 = V3 % V2 #show remainder
print(k)
```
1.5999999999999996

```
V5 = V2 ** 2
print(V5)
```
12.25

```
V5 = V2 ** V1
print(V5)
```
12.25

```
V5 = V1 + V2 * V3 - V4 # show BODMAS
print(V5)
```
13.099999999999998

```
V5 = (V1+ V2) * (V3 - V4)
print(V5)
```
-9.075000000000003

   2.
   2.1
```
1alist4a.py

list1 = [1,2,3,4,5,6,7]
print (list1)
for x in list1:
 print(x)
```

```
for x in range(7):
    new = int(input("Enter an integer: "))
    list1.append(new)
print(list1)
```

This outputs

```
[1, 2, 3, 4, 5, 6, 7]
1
2
3
4
5
6
7
Enter an integer: 58
Enter an integer: 2
Enter an integer: 3
Enter an integer: 4
Enter an integer: 5
Enter an integer: 6
Enter an integer: 7
[1, 2, 3, 4, 5, 6, 7, 58, 2, 3, 4, 5, 6, 7]
```

2.2

```
adict4a.py
in adict4a.py program
my_dict = {'a' : 'one', 'b' : 'two'}
print("Enter key to be tested: ")
testkey = input()
found = 0
```

```
for item in my_dict:
    if testkey in my_dict:
        print ("specified found")
        found = 1
        break
if found == 0:
    print ("specified not found")
```

This outputs (if you enter "a" when asked for a key)

Enter key to be tested:

a

specified found

or outputs (if you enter "x" when asked for a key)

Enter key to be tested:

x

specified not found

2.3

```
# Iterating over a tuple
tup1=(2,4,6,8,10,12,14)
for element in tup1:
 print (element)
```

2

4

6

8

10

12

14

3.

```
test5e.py
fileout = open("pjfileqi.bin", "w")
```

```
line1 = "a-Jones-D-37-accountant-45000\n"
fileout.write(line1)

line2 = "b-Smith-A-42-HR-55000 \n"
fileout.write(line2)

line3 = "c-Allen-R-28-Secretary-40000 \n"
fileout.write(line3)

line4 = "d-Bradley-S-26-Programmer-50000 \n"
fileout.write(line4)

fileout.close()

filein = open("pjfileqi.bin", "r")

a=filein.readline()
b=filein.readline()
c=filein.readline()
d=filein.readline()

print(a)
print(b)
print(c)
print(d)

filein.close()
```

When you run this program, its output is

a-Jones-D-37-accountant-45000

b-Smith-A-42-HR-55000

c-Allen-R-28-Secretary-40000

d-Bradley-S-26-Programmer-50000

```
a
a-Jones-D-37-accountant-45000
```

Chapter 2

1.   The code is as follows:

c1.2ex1.c

```
#define _CRT_SECURE_NO_WARNINGS
#include<stdio.h>
/* demonstrate a forloop (setting the forloop limit)*/
main()

{

    float this_is_a_number ,  total;
    int i,forlimit;

    total = 0;
    printf( "Please enter forloop limit:\n " );
            scanf( "%d", &forlimit );/* entered limit stored in forlimit */
    for(i=0;i<forlimit;i++)
    {

            printf( "Please enter a number:\n " );
            scanf( "%f", &this_is_a_number );
            total = total + this_is_a_number;

    }
    printf("Total Sum is = %f\n",total);

}
```

2.   The program for this is as follows:

c1.2ex2.c

```
    #include<stdio.h>

#define _CRT_SECURE_NO_WARNINGS
/* example of a 2D array test for 2 arrays*/
```

```c
int main()
{
    int arr1[8][8];
    int arr2[8][8];

    int i,j,k,l;

    printf("enter number of rows and columns of first array(max 8 rows max
    8 columns) \n");
    scanf("%d %d", &k, &l);
    if(k>8 || l>8)
    {
        printf("error - max of 8 for rows or columns\n");

    }

    else
    {
        printf("enter array\n");
        for(i=0;i<k;1++)
        {
            for(j=0;j<l;j++)
            {
                scanf("%d",&arr1[i][j]);
            }
        }
        printf("Your array is \n");
        for(i=0;i<k;i++)
        {
            for(j=0;j<l;j++)
            {
                printf("%d ",arr1[i][j]);
            }
        printf("\n");

        }
    }
```

```
printf("first row of first array\n");
for(j=0;j<k;j++)
{
    printf("%d ",arr1[0][j]);
}

printf("enter number of rows and columns of second array(max 8 rows
max 8 columns) \n");
scanf("%d %d", &k, &l);
if(k>8 || l>8)
{
    printf("error - max of 8 for rows or columns\n");

}

else
{
    printf("enter array\n");
    for(i=0;i<k;i++)
    {
        for(j=0;j<l;j++)
        {
            scanf("%d",&arr2[i][j]);
        }
    }
    printf("Your array is \n");
    for(i=0;i<k;i++)
    {
        for(j=0;j<l;j++)
        {
            printf("%d ",arr2[i][j]);
        }
    printf("\n");

    }
}
printf("first row of second array\n");
```

```
    for(j=0;j<k;j++)
            {
                    printf("%d ",arr2[0][j]);
            }
        printf("\n");
}
```

3. A program to do this is as follows:

c1.2ex3.c

```
/* Function which returns an answer   */
/* finds the pupil in one year of the school with the highest marks */

#include <stdio.h>
double getmarks(double pupils[]);

int main()
{
    double pupil;
    /* Array with marks for class is preset in the main part of the program */
    double  marks[] = {1.2,2.3,3.4,4.5,5.6,6.7,7.8,8.9,9.0};
    /* Call function getmarks. The function returns the average marks
    which is then stored in pupil */
    pupil = getmarks(marks);
    printf("Average mark is  = %lf", pupil);
    return 0;
}

double getmarks(double pupils[])
{
    int i;
    double average, total;
    total = 0;
    /* Go through all the pupils in turn and add their mark */
```

```
    for (i = 0; i < 9; ++i)
    {
        total = total + pupils[i];

    }
    average = total/9;
    return average; /* returns the value in average to where the function
    was called */
}
```

4. The code for this question is given in the following:

c1.2ex4.c

```
#define _CRT_SECURE_NO_WARNINGS
#include<stdio.h>

/*appends a record to the file*/
/* then prints the whole file */

/*define the structure for each student's data */

struct student {
    int studentID;
    char name[13];
    int marks;
};

int main()
{
    int i, numread;
    FILE *fp;
    struct student s1;
    struct student s2;

    /* Preset the data for the student */

    struct student s25 = { 25,"Foster       ",82 };
```

```c
/* Open the students file */
fp = fopen("students.bin", "a");

/* Write details of the student to file*/
/* From the structure defined above */

fwrite(&s25, sizeof(s1), 1, fp);

/* Close the file */

fclose(fp);

/* Reopen the file */

fopen("students.bin", "r");

/* Read and print out all of the records on the file */
for (i = 0;i < 16;i++)
{

    numread = fread(&s2, sizeof(s2), 1, fp);/* read into structure s2 */

    if (numread == 1)
    {

    /* reference elements of structure by s2.studentID etc */
        printf("\nstudentID : %d", s2.studentID);
        printf("\nName : %s", s2.name);
        printf("\nmarks : %d", s2.marks);
    }
    else {
        /* If an error occurred on read then print out message */

        if (feof(fp))

            printf("Error reading students.bin : unexpected end of
            file fp is %p\n", fp);
```

```
            else if (ferror(fp))
            {
                    perror("Error reading students.bin");
            }
        }
    }
    /* Close the file */

    fclose(fp);

}
```

Chapter 3

1. The following program inserts a number of rows and asks the user
    to enter the details of each row:

Csqlinsert_manyx.c

```
#include <sqlite3.h>
#include <stdio.h>
int main(void)
{
    sqlite3 *db;
    char *err_msg = 0;

    /* storage areas for user-inserted id, name, age and occupation */
int idin,agein,rowsin,i;
    char namein[13];
    char occupin[15];

    int rc = sqlite3_open("test.db", &db); /* test the database is there */
    if (rc != SQLITE_OK)
    {
        fprintf(stderr, "Cannot open database: %s\n",
        sqlite3_errmsg(db));
        sqlite3_close(db);
```

```
        return 1;
    }

    /* Ask the user to enter the number of rows */
    /* they wish to insert */

printf("enter the number of rows you wish to insert (max      10) \n");
    scanf("%d", &rowsin);

    /* Use a forloop to enter each row during one loop of the forloop */

    for(i=0; i<rowsin; i++)
    {

        /* Ask the user to enter the ID, Name, */
        /* age and occupation for the current insert */

        printf("enter  id \n");
        scanf("%d", &idin);
        printf("enter name id \n");
        scanf("%s", &namein);
        printf("enter age \n");
        scanf("%d", &agein);
        printf("enter occupation \n");
        scanf("%s", &occupin);

        /* Create the INSERT string */

        char str1[200] = "INSERT INTO Personnel VALUES( ";
        char str2[] = " ); ";
        char str3[2];
        char str4[6];
        char str5[] = ", ";
        char str6[] = "'";

        sprintf(str4, "%d", idin);
        sprintf(str3, "%d", agein);
```

```
        strcat(str1,str4);
        strcat(str1,str5);
        strcat(str1,str6);
        strcat(str1,namein);
        strcat(str1,str6);
        strcat(str1,str5);
        strcat(str1,str3);
        strcat(str1,str5);
        strcat(str1,str6);
        strcat(str1,occupin);
        strcat(str1,str6);
        strcat(str1,str2);

        printf(str1);
        printf("\n");

        char *sql = str1; /* store the string in *sql */

        rc = sqlite3_exec(db, sql, 0, 0, &err_msg);/*perform one insert */
        if (rc != SQLITE_OK )
        {
            fprintf(stderr, "SQL error: %s\n", err_msg);
            sqlite3_free(err_msg);
            sqlite3_close(db);
            return 1;
        }
    }
    sqlite3_close(db);
    return 0;
}
```

You can check if your inserts have worked by running the program **Csqlselect_allx2c** which prints out all of the rows in the table.

2. Your code should be something like this:

```c
/* csqlfilereadins2.c */

/* reads from file */
/* reads and prints sequentially */
/* reads and prints specific records */
#define _CRT_SECURE_NO_WARNINGS

#include <sqlite3.h>
#include <stdio.h>
int main(void)
{
struct Employee
{
        int ID;
        char name[13];
        int age;
        char occup[15];
};
FILE *fp;
    struct Employee s2;
    int numread, i;

int count;
    sqlite3 *db;
    char *err_msg = 0;

    int idin,agein;
    char namein[13];
    char occupin[15];

    int rc = sqlite3_open("test.db", &db);/* open the database */
    if (rc != SQLITE_OK)
    {
        fprintf(stderr, "Cannot open database: %s\n",
        sqlite3_errmsg(db));
        sqlite3_close(db);
        return 1;
    }
```

```
char *sql = "DROP TABLE IF EXISTS Personnel;"
"CREATE TABLE Personnel(Id INT PRIMARY KEY, Name TEXT,        Age INT,
Occupation);";

rc = sqlite3_exec(db, sql, 0, 0, &err_msg); /*creates the table */

 if (rc != SQLITE_OK )
 {
     fprintf(stderr, "SQL error: %s\n", err_msg);
     sqlite3_free(err_msg);
     sqlite3_close(db);
     return 1;
 }

count = 0;

/* Open People3 file */

fp = fopen("People3.bin", "r");
for (i = 0;i < 11;i++)
{
    /* Read each People3 data from file sequentially */
    fread(&s2, sizeof(s2), 1, fp);
    count++;

    /* Insert each field read into the table */
    idin = s2.ID;

    strcpy(namein, s2.name);

    agein = s2.age;

    strcpy(occupin, s2.occup);

    printf("id is %d:name is %s:age is %d:occupation is %s\n",idin,
    namein, agein, occupin);

    /* The INSERT command string is set up */

    char str1[200] = "INSERT INTO Personnel VALUES( ";
    char str2[] = " ); ";
    char str3[2];
```

```c
        char str4[6];
        char str5[] = ", ";
        char str6[] = "'";

        sprintf(str4, "%d", idin);
        sprintf(str3, "%d", agein);

        strcat(str1,str4); /* ID */
        strcat(str1,str5); /* comma */
        strcat(str1,str6); /* quote */
        strcat(str1,namein); /* name */
        strcat(str1,str6); /* quote */
        strcat(str1,str5); /* comma */
        strcat(str1,str3); /* age */
        strcat(str1,str5); /* comma */
        strcat(str1,str6); /* quote */
        strcat(str1,occupin); /* occupation */
        strcat(str1,str6); /* quote */
        strcat(str1,str2); /* close bracket and semi-colon */

        printf(str1); /* completed string */
/* so, for ID=12, name=Pickford, age=48 and occupation = Welder */
/* our completed string will be :- */
/* INSERT INTO Personnel VALUES( 12, 'Pickford', 48, 'Welder' ); */

        char *sql = str1;
        printf("\n");

        rc = sqlite3_exec(db, sql, 0, 0, &err_msg);/* execute the insert */
        if (rc != SQLITE_OK )
        {
            fprintf(stderr, "SQL error: %s\n", err_msg);
            sqlite3_free(err_msg);
            sqlite3_close(db);
            return 1;
        }
    }
```

```
    printf("count is %d\n",count);
    sqlite3_close(db); /* close the database connection */

    fclose(fp);
    return 0;
}
```

The program should read 11 records from the People3 file and print out the following (for each record, the first line is the record read from the file, and the next line is the corresponding INSERT command to insert that data into the table):

```
id is 10:name is Brown :age is 50:occupation is accountant
INSERT INTO Personnel VALUES( 10, 'Brown ', 50, 'accountant' );
id is 11:name is Jones :age is 51:occupation is programmer
INSERT INTO Personnel VALUES( 11, 'Jones ', 51, 'programmer' );
id is 12:name is White :age is 52:occupation is engineer
INSERT INTO Personnel VALUES( 12, 'White ', 52, 'engineer' );
id is 13:name is Green :age is 53:occupation is electrician
INSERT INTO Personnel VALUES( 13, 'Green ', 53, 'electrician' );
id is 14:name is Smith :age is 54:occupation is joiner
INSERT INTO Personnel VALUES( 14, 'Smith ', 54, 'joiner' );
id is 15:name is Black :age is 55:occupation is programmer
INSERT INTO Personnel VALUES( 15, 'Black ', 55, 'programmer' );
id is 16:name is Allen :age is 56:occupation is secretary
INSERT INTO Personnel VALUES( 16, 'Allen ', 56, 'secretary' );
id is 17:name is Stone :age is 57:occupation is manager
INSERT INTO Personnel VALUES( 17, 'Stone ', 57, 'manager' );
id is 18:name is Evans :age is 58:occupation is receptionist
INSERT INTO Personnel VALUES( 18, 'Evans ', 58, 'receptionist' );
id is 19:name is Royle :age is 59:occupation is engineer
INSERT INTO Personnel VALUES( 19, 'Royle ', 59, 'engineer' );
id is 20:name is Stone :age is 60:occupation is cleaner
INSERT INTO Personnel VALUES( 20, 'Stone ', 60, 'cleaner' );
count is 11
```

You can check if your inserts have worked by running the program **Csqlselect_allx2c** which prints out all of the rows in the table.

Chapter 4

1. **pysqlite70cretwo.py** OK (multiple rows to two different tables)

```
import sqlite3

conn = sqlite3.connect('staff.db')
cur = conn.cursor()
print ("Opened database successfully")

cur.execute('DROP TABLE IF EXISTS staff')
cur.execute('CREATE TABLE staff (id INTEGER, name TEXT, initial, gender
TEXT, age INTEGER, occup TEXT)')

cur.execute('INSERT INTO staff (id, name, initial, gender, age, occup)
VALUES (?, ?, ?, ?, ?, ?)',
    (1, 'Jones', 'A', 'M', 23, 'Accountant'))
cur.execute('INSERT INTO staff (id, name, initial, gender, age, occup)
VALUES (?, ?, ?, ?, ?, ?)',
    (2, 'Smith', 'J', 'M', 47, 'Salesman'))
cur.execute('INSERT INTO staff (id, name, initial, gender, age, occup)
VALUES (?, ?, ?, ?, ?, ?)',
    (3, 'Zeiss', 'H', 'F', 38, 'Architect'))
cur.execute('INSERT INTO staff (id, name, initial, gender, age, occup)
VALUES (?, ?, ?, ?, ?, ?)',
    (4, 'Blaine', 'S', 'F', 28, 'SE'))
cur.execute('INSERT INTO staff (id, name, initial, gender, age, occup)
VALUES (?, ?, ?, ?, ?, ?)',
    (5, 'Postlethwaite', 'D', 'M', 63, 'Advisor'))
cur.execute('INSERT INTO staff (id, name, initial, gender, age, occup)
VALUES (?, ?, ?, ?, ?, ?)',
    (6, 'Junkers', 'A', 'M', 59, 'Designer'))

print('staff:')
cur.execute('SELECT id, name, initial, gender, age, occup FROM staff')
for row in cur:
    print(row)
```

```
conn.commit()

cur.execute('DROP TABLE IF EXISTS supply')
cur.execute('CREATE TABLE supply (id INTEGER, coname TEXT, address TEXT,
type TEXT)')

cur.execute('INSERT INTO supply (id, coname, address, type) VALUES (?, ?,
?, ?)',
    (1, 'Lenox Co.', '95th Street', 'Concrete'))
cur.execute('INSERT INTO supply (id, coname, address, type) VALUES (?, ?,
?, ?)',
    (2, 'City Builders', 'Avon Ave', 'Bricks'))
cur.execute('INSERT INTO supply (id, coname, address, type) VALUES (?, ?,
?, ?)',
    (3, 'Portway', 'New Strand', 'Windows'))
cur.execute('INSERT INTO supply (id, coname, address, type) VALUES (?, ?,
?, ?)',
    (4, 'Huygens Inc', 'Corona Drive', 'Wood panelling'))

print('supply:')
cur.execute('SELECT id, coname, address, type FROM supply')
for row in cur:
    print(row)

conn.commit()

conn.close()
```

The output from this program is

```
Opened database successfully
staff:
(1, 'Jones', 'A', 'M', 23, 'Accountant')
(2, 'Smith', 'J', 'M', 47, 'Salesman')
(3, 'Zeiss', 'H', 'F', 38, 'Architect')
(4, 'Blaine', 'S', 'F', 28, 'SE')
(5, 'Postlethwaite', 'D', 'M', 63, 'Advisor')
(6, 'Junkers', 'A', 'M', 59, 'Designer')
```

supply:
```
(1, 'Lenox Co.', '95th Street', 'Concrete')
(2, 'City Builders', 'Avon Ave', 'Bricks')
(3, 'Portway', 'New Strand', 'Windows')
(4, 'Huygens Inc', 'Corona Drive', 'Wood panelling')
```

2. This is just a matter of commenting out the "break" from the while loop so that you can insert as many rows as you want to, until you enter 'quit' when asked for the next name.

pysqlite63cind.py

```python
#!/usr/bin/python

import sqlite3

conn = sqlite3.connect('Personnel.db')
cur = conn.cursor()
print ("Opened database successfully")

while True:
    acct = input('Enter an name, or quit: ')

    if(acct == 'quit'): break
    idin = input('Enter ID: ')
    initial = input('Enter initial: ')
    gender = input('Enter gender: ')
    agein = input('Enter age: ')
    occup = input('Enter occupation: ')

    cur.execute('INSERT INTO Personnel (id, name, initial, gender, age, occup)
    VALUES (?, ?, ?, ?, ?, ?)',(idin, acct, initial, gender, agein, occup))
    #break THIS IS THE ONLY CHANGE TO THE PROGRAM. WHEN YOU ARE
    # ASKED to 'Enter an name, or quit: ' at the start of the while
    # loop then entering 'quit' exits from the loop, so you can enter
    # as many rows as you want.
```

```
print('Personnel:')
cur.execute('SELECT id, name, initial, gender, age, occup FROM Personnel')
for row in cur:
    print(row)

conn.commit()

conn.close()
```

If you run this program and enter data for three people to be added to the file with IDs of 42, 43, and 44, you will get the following:

```
Opened database successfully
Enter an name, or quit: Price
Enter ID: 42
Enter initial: D
Enter gender: M
Enter age: 54
Enter occupation: Storeman
Enter an name, or quit: Short
Enter ID: 43
Enter initial: L
Enter gender: F
Enter age: 43
Enter occupation: Secretary
Enter an name, or quit: Newell
Enter ID: 44
Enter initial: S
Enter gender: F
Enter age: 36
Enter occupation: Engineer
Enter an name, or quit: quit
Personnel:
(1, 'Jones', 'A', 'M', 23, 'Accountant')
(2, 'Smith', 'J', 'M', 28, 'Salesman')
(11, 'Jones', 'A', 'M', 23, 'Accountant')
(12, 'Smith', 'J', 'M', 28, 'Salesman')
```

```
(13, 'Zeiss', 'H', 'F', 38, 'Architect')
(15, 'Postlethwaite', 'D', 'M', 63, 'Advisor')
(16, 'Junkers', 'A', 'M', 38, 'Designer')
(21, 'Robinson', 'C', 'F', 31, 'Engineer')
(25, 'Van der Kirchoff', 'I', 'M', 34, 'plumber')
(42, 'Price', 'D', 'M', 54, 'Storeman')
(43, 'Short', 'L', 'F', 43, 'Secretary')
(44, 'Newell', 'S', 'F', 36, 'Engineer')
```

Chapter 5

1.

histex.c

```c
/*Histogram Program*/
#define _CRT_SECURE_NO_WARNINGS
#define PY_SSIZE_T_CLEAN
#include <stdio.h>
#include <math.h>
#include <conio.h>
#include "include/Python.h"

main()
{
    int marks[20];

    int i;

    char filename[] = "pyex3a.py";
    FILE* fp2;

    FILE *fp;
    FILE *fp3;

    fp=fopen("histn.bin","w");

    /* User enters 20 marks for a histogram*/
    printf("enter 20 marks (\n");
```

```c
    /* User enters marks*/
    for (i = 0;i < 20;i++)
    {
        printf("marks");
        scanf("%d", &marks[i]);

    }

    /* Print the marks entered */
    printf("marks are \n");
    for (i = 0;i < 20;i++)
    {
        printf(" \n");
        printf("%d ", marks[i]);
        fprintf(fp,"%d\n",marks[i]);
    }
    printf(" \n");

fclose(fp);

Py_Initialize();

    fp2 = _Py_fopen(filename, "r");
    PyRun_SimpleFile(fp2, filename);

    Py_Finalize();


}
```

pyex3a.py

```python
import matplotlib.pyplot as plt
import numpy as np

# Read data from histn.bin file

x = np.loadtxt("histn.bin")
print("Data read from histn.bin")
print("x = ",x)
```

```
# Set up the arrays for the graph

xvals = [0]*20 #length of array is num. of coords entered

zint = 20
# set up the x array from the values entered
for b in range(zint):
    a = x[b]
    xvals[b] = a

# Print the x and y values to the user

print("xvals = ",xvals)

number_of_bins = 10

n = plt.hist(xvals, number_of_bins, facecolor='blue')

print("Counts in each bin")
print(n[0]) # counts in each bin

# Display the graph

plt.xlabel('marks (%)')
plt.ylabel('Number of Students')
plt.title('Histogram Exam Marks')
plt.show()
```

If you run histex and enter the marks as shown, this will be the output

enter 20 marks (
marks51
marks23
marks18
marks59
marks6
marks71
marks48
marks69
marks60
marks39

marks45
marks63
marks64
marks45
marks36
marks97
marks18
marks49
marks50
marks90
marks are

51
23
18
59
6
71
48
69
60
39
45
63
64
45
36
97
18
49
50
90
Data read from histn.bin
y = [51. 23. 18. 59. 6. 71. 48. 69. 60. 39. 45. 63. 64. 45. 36. 97. 18.
49. 50. 90.]

```
xvals =  [51.0, 23.0, 18.0, 59.0, 6.0, 71.0, 48.0, 69.0, 60.0, 39.0, 45.0,
63.0, 64.0, 45.0, 36.0, 97.0, 18.0, 49.0, 50.0, 90.0]
[1. 3. 0. 2. 6. 2. 3. 1. 0. 2.]
[ 6.   15.1 24.2 33.3 42.4 51.5 60.6 69.7 78.8 87.9 97. ]
<a list of 10 Patch objects>
```

with the following histogram:

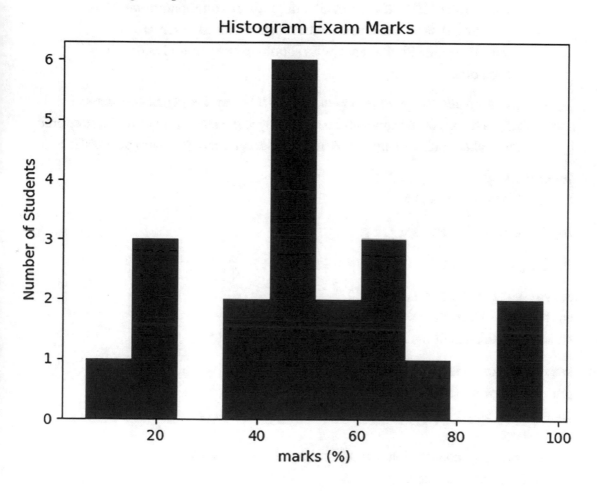

Chapter 6

1. The first server and client pair are shown in the following. The second server and client pair should be exactly the same as the first two except that they have a different port to the first two. The first server-client pair have port 1000, so give the second server-client pair a port of 1001. If you run all four programs on separate windows, you should be able to do a concurrent chat with each server-client pair. The pair with the same ports should only communicate with each other.

This program allows the server-client pairs to be created and run concurrently. socsert2x.py is the server program and socclit2x.py is the client program. There should be one server-client pair with port 1000 and one server-client pair with port 1001.

Socsert2x.py

```
# Socket Server Program

import time, socket, sys

server_port = 1000

server_socket = socket.socket()
host_name = socket.gethostname()
server_socket.bind((host_name ,server_port))

server_socket.listen(1)
print ("Server is loaded")
connection_socket, address = server_socket.accept()
while True:
    sentence = connection_socket.recv(2048).decode()
    print('>> ',sentence)
    message = input(">> ")
    connection_socket.send(message.encode())
```

```
    if(message == 'windup'):
        connection_socket.close()
        break
```

Socclit2x.py

```
# Socket Client Program

import time, socket, sys

server_name = socket.gethostname()
server_port = 1000

client_socket = socket.socket()
host_name = socket.gethostname()

client_socket.connect((server_name,server_port))
while True:
    sentence = input(">> ")
    client_socket.send(sentence.encode())
    message = client_socket.recv(2048)
    print (">> ", message.decode())
    if(sentence == 'windup'):
        client_socket.close()
        break
```

Index

A

accept command, 185
Algebra rules, 5
Amend age, 125, 127
Arithmetic operations, 3
Array
    append, 11
    delete, 10
    insert, 8, 9
    search, 10
    update, 11

B

bind command, 185

C

close command, 185
connect command, 185
conn.total_changes, 141
C programming language
    adding two integers, 60, 62
    data arrays, 70–72, 74, 75, 77–81, 106
    do while loops, 65
    file access, 94
    functions, 81–86
    Goto command, 92
    if else, 67, 68
    if else if, 68, 70
    for loops, 63, 64
    mathematical/logical symbols, 93

multiply/divide two numbers, 62
printf, 60
size of variables, 91
strings, 86
structures, 88, 89, 91
switch instructions, 66

D

Data types, 2
DELETE command, 133
Delete rows, 128, 130
Dictionaries, 17
    amend, 18
    append, 17
    create, 17
    delete, 19
    search, 19

E

Embedded Python
    enter data to plot, 160–169
    histogram, 177, 178
    importing picture, 179, 180
    mechanisms, 151, 153
    plot 2D line, 153–155
    plot trigonometric curves, 158–160
    plot two 2D lines, 155–157
    Python code, 151
    2D center, mass plot, 170–175, 177
encode() command, 185
execute command, 133

P. Joyce, *C and Python Applications*, https://doi.org/10.1007/978-1-4842-7774-4

F

feof(fp), 95
File access, 45, 47, 49, 51
    fclose, 94
    fopen, 94
    student records file
        file update, 100–105
        fread, 98, 99
        numread, 95–97
        structure, 95
fopen command, 94

G

getchar and putchar instructions, 60
gethostname, 186
getmarks, 86

H

Handshaking, 183

I, J, K

if statements, 25
import instruction, 183
#include<stdio.h>, 59
INSERT INTO command, 134
Inserts row
    preset row, 113
    user-entered row, 114, 116

L

line.split() function, 46
list(range(0,100,10)) function, 156
Lists, 14
    append, 16

    delete, 16
    reading entries, 15
    update, 16
for loop, 26, 27
Loops
    for loop, 26, 27
    while loop, 28

M

Mathematical functions, 42
matmul function, 37
matplotlib and numpy, 151
matplotlib.pyplot, 38
Matrix arithmetic, 31
Multiplying matrices, 33

N, O, P, Q

Numpy, 30
    calculation, 34, 36, 37

R

Regression, 52, 54–56

S

SELECT command, 144, 147
Select row
    age, 122, 124, 125
    all, 120, 121
    preset, 117, 119
Socket
    chat programs, 197, 198
    client-server, 185, 187
    definition, 183
    main code calls, 184
    server-client mechanism, 184

server-client pair send/receive
file, 187, 189, 190
TCP/IP, 183
threaded server, closing down, 194–196
threaded system, 191–193
strcat, 88
strcmp, 88
strcpy, 88
string.h library, 86
Strings, 12, 14
strlen, 88
Structured Query Language (SQL), 107
create database, 108–110
create table, 110, 112, 113, 133
definition, 131
delete row, 148
inserting row, mechanisms, 134
insert two preset rows, 135
six preset rows, 136, 137
user, 138
read table, 149
SQLite, 107
sqlite3, 132
typical database table, 131
update row
descending order, age, 146
insert/update, 143
preset, 139, 140
select row, 144
user, 141, 142
user-entered row, 145
user-entered select, age, 147
Switch, 29

T
tasklist command, 194
Tuples, 20, 21
concatenating 2
tuples, 22
convert list/string, 23
create, 21
create nested
tuples, 22
create repeated
tuples, 22
create variable, 24
delete, 24
reading, 23
search, 23
single-element tuple, 23

U
UPDATE command, 133, 139
User-written functions, 43, 44

V
Variables, 1
characters, 6
reading data, 6–8
real (Float) numbers, 5
types, 2

W, X, Y, Z
while loop, 28

Printed in the United States
by Baker & Taylor Publisher Services